**W9-CCI-096**

*Clifford R. O'Donnell*
*Editor*

# Culture, Peers, and Delinquency

*Culture, Peers, and Delinquency* has been co-published simultaneously as *Journal of Prevention & Intervention in the Community*, Volume 25, Number 2 2003.

*Pre-publication*
*REVIEWS,*
*COMMENTARIES,*
*EVALUATIONS . . .*

"TIMELY. . . . OF VALUE TO BOTH STUDENTS AND PROFESSIONALS. . . . Demonstrates how peers can serve as a pathway to delinquency from a multiethnic perspective. The discussion of ethnic, racial, and gender differences challenges the field to reconsider assessment, treatment, and preventative approaches."

**Donald Meichenbaum, PhD**
*Distinguished Professor Emeritus*
*University of Waterloo*
*Ontario, Canada;*
*Research Director*
*The Melissa Institute for Violence Prevention and the Treatment of Victims of Violence*
*Miami, Florida*

The Haworth Press, Inc.

# Culture, Peers, and Delinquency

*Culture, Peers, and Delinquency* has been co-published simultaneously as *Journal of Prevention & Intervention in the Community*, Volume 25, Number 2 2003.

Tel: (773) 325-4244
Fax: (773) 325-7888
E-mail: jferrari@depaul.edu

Journal of
Prevention & Intervention in the Community

**Editor: Joseph R. Ferrari, PhD**
Professor
Department of Psychology
DePaul University
2219 N. Kenmore Avenue
Chicago, IL 60614-3504

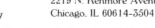 **The Haworth Press**, Inc., 10 Alice Street, Binghamton, NY 13904-1580 USA

The *Journal of Prevention & Intervention in the Community*™ Monographic "Separates" (formerly the *Prevention in Human Services* series)*

For information on previous issues of *Prevention in Human Services*, edited by Robert E. Hess, please contact: The Haworth Press, Inc., 10 Alice Street, Binghamton, NY 13904-1580 USA.

Below is a list of "separates," which in serials librarianship means a special issue simultaneously published as a special journal issue or double-issue *and* as a "separate" hardbound monograph. (This is a format which we also call a "DocuSerial.")

"Separates" are published because specialized libraries or professionals may wish to purchase a specific thematic issue by itself in a format which can be separately cataloged and shelved, as opposed to purchasing the journal on an on-going basis. Faculty members may also more easily consider a "separate" for classroom adoption.

"Separates" are carefully classified separately with the major book jobbers so that the journal tie-in can be noted on new book order slips to avoid duplicate purchasing.

You may wish to visit Haworth's website at . . .

### http://www.HaworthPress.com

. . . to search our online catalog for complete tables of contents of these separates and related publications.

You may also call 1-800-HAWORTH (outside US/Canada: 607-722-5857), or Fax 1-800-895-0582 (outside US/Canada: 607-771-0012), or e-mail at:

### docdelivery@haworthpress.com

---

**Culture, Peers, and Delinquency,** edited by Clifford O'Donnell, PhD (Vol. 25, No. 2, 2003). *"TIMELY .... OF VALUE TO BOTH STUDENTS AND PROFESSIONALS. . . . Demonstrates how peers can serve as a pathway to delinquency from a multiethnic perspective. The discussion of ethnic, racial, and gender differences challenges the field to reconsider assessment, treatment, and preventative approaches." (Donald Meichenbaum, PhD, Distinguished Professor Emeritus, University of Waterloo, Ontario, Canada; Research Director, The Melissa Institute for Violence Prevention and the Treatment of Victims of Violence, Miami, Florida)*

**Prevention and Intervention Practice in Post-Apartheid South Africa,** edited by Vijé Franchi, PhD, and Norman Duncan, PhD, consulting editor (Vol. 25, No.1, 2003). *"Highlights the way in which preventive and curative interventions serve–or do not serve–the ideals of equality, empowerment, and participation. . . . Revolutionizes our way of thinking about and teaching socio-pedagogical action in the context of exclusion." (Dr. Altay A. Manço, Scientific Director, Institute of Research, Training, and Action on Migrations, Belgium)*

**Community Interventions to Create Change in Children,** edited by Lorna H. London, PhD (Vol. 24, No. 2, 2002). *"ILLUSTRATES CREATIVE APPROACHES to prevention and intervention with at-risk youth. . . . Describes multiple methods to consider in the design, implementation, and evaluation of programs." (Susan D. McMahon, PhD, Assistant Professor, Department of Psychology, DePaul University)*

**Preventing Youth Access to Tobacco,** edited by Leonard A. Jason, PhD, and Steven B. Pokorny, PhD (Vol. 24, No. 1, 2002). *"Explores cutting-edge issues in youth access research methodology. . . . Provides a thorough review of the tobacco control literature and detailed analysis of the methodological issues presented by community interventions to increase the effectiveness of tobacco control. . . . Challenges widespread assumptions about the dynamics of youth access programs and the requirements for long-term success." (John A. Gardiner, PhD, LLB, Consultant to the 2000 Surgeon General's Report* Reducing Youth Access to Tobacco *and to the National Cancer Institute's evaluation of the ASSIST program)*

**The Transition from Welfare to Work: Processes, Challenges, and Outcomes,** edited by Sharon Telleen, PhD, and Judith V. Sayad (Vol. 23, No. 1/2, 2002). *A comprehensive examination of the welfare-to-work initiatives surrounding the major reform of United States welfare legislation in 1996.*

***Prevention Issues for Women's Health in the New Millennium***, edited by Wendee M. Wechsberg, PhD (Vol. 22, No. 2, 2001). *"Helpful to service providers as well as researchers . . . A USEFUL ANCILLARY TEXTBOOK for courses addressing women's health issues. Covers a wide range of health issues affecting women." (Sherry Deren, PhD, Director, Center for Drug Use and HIV Research, National Drug Research Institute, New York City)*

***Workplace Safety: Individual Differences in Behavior***, edited by Alice F. Stuhlmacher, PhD, and Douglas F. Cellar, PhD (Vol. 22, No. 1, 2001). Workplace Safety: Individual Differences in Behavior *examines safety behavior and outlines practical interventions to help increase safety awareness. Individual differences are relevant to a variety of settings, including the workplace, public spaces, and motor vehicles. This book takes a look at ways of defining and measuring safety as well as a variety of individual differences like gender, job knowledge, conscientiousness, self-efficacy, risk avoidance, and stress tolerance that are important in creating safety interventions and improving the selection and training of employees.* Workplace Safety *takes an incisive look at these issues with a unique focus on the way individual differences in people impact safety behavior in the real world.*

***People with Disabilities: Empowerment and Community Action,*** edited by Christopher B. Keys, PhD, and Peter W. Dowrick, PhD (Vol. 21, No. 2, 2001). *"Timely and useful . . . provides valuable lessons and guidance for everyone involved in the disability movement. This book is a must-read for researchers and practitioners interested in disability rights issues!" (Karen M. Ward, EdD, Director, Center for Human Development; Associate Professor, University of Alaska, Anchorage)*

***Family Systems/Family Therapy: Applications for Clinical Practice***, edited by Joan D. Atwood, PhD (Vol. 21, No. 1, 2001). *Examines family therapy issues in the context of the larger systems of health, law, and education and suggests ways family therapists can effectively use an intersystems approach.*

***HIV/AIDS Prevention: Current Issues in Community Practice***, edited by Doreen D. Salina, PhD (Vol. 19, No. 1, 2000). *Helps researchers and psychologists explore specific methods of improving HIV/AIDS prevention research.*

***Educating Students to Make-a-Difference: Community-Based Service Learning,*** edited by Joseph R. Ferrari, PhD, and Judith G. Chapman, PhD (Vol. 18, No. 1/2, 1999). *"There is something here for everyone interested in the social psychology of service-learning." (Frank Bernt, PhD, Associate Professor, St. Joseph's University)*

***Program Implementation in Preventive Trials,*** edited by Joseph A. Durlak and Joseph R. Ferrari, PhD (Vol. 17, No. 2, 1998). *"Fills an important gap in preventive research. . . . Highlights an array of important questions related to implementation and demonstrates just how good community-based intervention programs can be when issues related to implementation are taken seriously." (Judy Primavera, PhD, Associate Professor of Psychology, Fairfield University, Fairfield, Connecticut)*

***Preventing Drunk Driving,*** edited by Elsie R. Shore, PhD, and Joseph R. Ferrari, PhD (Vol. 17, No. 1, 1998). *"A must read for anyone interested in reducing the needless injuries and death caused by the drunk driver." (Terrance D. Schiavone, President, National Commission Against Drunk Driving, Washington, DC)*

***Manhood Development in Urban African-American Communities,*** edited by Roderick J. Watts, PhD, and Robert J. Jagers (Vol. 16, No. 1/2, 1998). *"Watts and Jagers provide the much-needed foundational and baseline information and research that begins to philosophically and empirically validate the importance of understanding culture, oppression, and gender when working with males in urban African-American communities." (Paul Hill, Jr., MSW, LISW, ACSW, East End Neighborhood House, Cleveland, Ohio)*

***Diversity Within the Homeless Population: Implications for Intervention,*** edited by Elizabeth M. Smith, PhD, and Joseph R. Ferrari, PhD (Vol. 15, No. 2, 1997). *"Examines why homelessness is increasing, as well as treatment options, case management techniques, and community intervention programs that can be used to prevent homelessness." (American Public Welfare Association)*

***Education in Community Psychology: Models for Graduate and Undergraduate Programs,*** edited by Clifford R. O'Donnell, PhD, and Joseph R. Ferrari, PhD (Vol. 15, No. 1, 1997). *"An invaluable resource for students seeking graduate training in community psychology . . . [and will] also serve faculty who want to improve undergraduate teaching and graduate programs." (Marybeth Shinn, PhD, Professor of Psychology and Coordinator, Community Doctoral Program, New York University, New York, New York)*

***Adolescent Health Care: Program Designs and Services,*** edited by John S. Wodarski, PhD, Marvin D. Feit, PhD, and Joseph R. Ferrari, PhD (Vol. 14, No. 1/2, 1997). *Devoted to helping practitioners address the problems of our adolescents through the use of preventive interventions based on sound empirical data.*

***Preventing Illness Among People with Coronary Heart Disease,*** edited by John D. Piette, PhD, Robert M. Kaplan, PhD, and Joseph R. Ferrari, PhD (Vol. 13, No. 1/2, 1996). *"A useful contribution to the interaction of physical health, mental health, and the behavioral interventions for patients with CHD." (Public Health: The Journal of the Society of Public Health)*

***Sexual Assault and Abuse: Sociocultural Context of Prevention,*** edited by Carolyn F. Swift, PhD* (Vol. 12, No. 2, 1995). *"Delivers a cornucopia for all who are concerned with the primary prevention of these damaging and degrading acts." (George J. McCall, PhD, Professor of Sociology and Public Administration, University of Missouri)*

***International Approaches to Prevention in Mental Health and Human Services,*** edited by Robert E. Hess, PhD, and Wolfgang Stark* (Vol. 12, No. 1, 1995). *Increases knowledge of prevention strategies from around the world.*

***Self-Help and Mutual Aid Groups: International and Multicultural Perspectives,*** edited by Francine Lavoie, PhD, Thomasina Borkman, PhD, and Benjamin Gidron* (Vol. 11, No. 1/2, 1995). *"A helpful orientation and overview, as well as useful data and methodological suggestions." (International Journal of Group Psychotherapy)*

***Prevention and School Transitions,*** edited by Leonard A. Jason, PhD, Karen E. Danner, and Karen S. Kurasaki, MA* (Vol. 10, No. 2, 1994). *"A collection of studies by leading ecological and systems-oriented theorists in the area of school transitions, describing the stressors, personal resources available, and coping strategies among different groups of children and adolescents undergoing school transitions." (Reference & Research Book News)*

***Religion and Prevention in Mental Health: Research, Vision, and Action,*** edited by Kenneth I. Pargament, PhD, Kenneth I. Maton, PhD, and Robert E. Hess, PhD* (Vol. 9, No. 2 & Vol. 10, No. 1, 1992). *"The authors provide an admirable framework for considering the important, yet often overlooked, differences in theological perspectives." (Family Relations)*

***Families as Nurturing Systems: Support Across the Life Span,*** edited by Donald G. Unger, PhD, and Douglas R. Powell, PhD* (Vol. 9, No. 1, 1991). *"A useful book for anyone thinking about alternative ways of delivering a mental health service." (British Journal of Psychiatry)*

***Ethical Implications of Primary Prevention,*** edited by Gloria B. Levin, PhD, and Edison J. Trickett, PhD* (Vol. 8, No. 2, 1991). *"A thoughtful and thought-provoking summary of ethical issues related to intervention programs and community research." (Betty Tableman, MPA, Director, Division. of Prevention Services and Demonstration Projects, Michigan Department of Mental Health, Lansing) Here is the first systematic and focused treatment of the ethical implications of primary prevention practice and research.*

***Career Stress in Changing Times,*** edited by James Campbell Quick, PhD, MBA, Robert E. Hess, PhD, Jared Hermalin, PhD, and Jonathan D. Quick, MD* (Vol. 8, No. 1, 1990). *"A well-organized book. . . . It deals with planning a career and career changes and the stresses involved." (American Association of Psychiatric Administrators)*

***Prevention in Community Mental Health Centers,*** edited by Robert E. Hess, PhD, and John Morgan, PhD* (Vol. 7, No. 2, 1990). *"A fascinating bird's-eye view of six significant programs of preventive care which have survived the rise and fall of preventive psychiatry in the U.S." (British Journal of Psychiatry)*

***Protecting the Children: Strategies for Optimizing Emotional and Behavioral Development,*** edited by Raymond P. Lorion, PhD* (Vol. 7, No. 1, 1990). *"This is a masterfully conceptualized and*

*edited volume presenting theory-driven, empirically based, developmentally oriented preven-
tion." (Michael C. Roberts, PhD, Professor of Psychology, The University of Alabama)*

**The National Mental Health Association: Eighty Years of Involvement in the Field of Prevention,**
edited by Robert E. Hess, PhD, and Jean DeLeon, PhD* (Vol. 6, No. 2, 1989). *"As a family life
educator interested in both the history of the field, current efforts, and especially the evaluation
of programs, I find this book quite interesting. I enjoyed reviewing it and believe that I will return to it many times. It is also a book I will recommend to students." (Family Relations)*

**A Guide to Conducting Prevention Research in the Community: First Steps,** by James G. Kelly,
PhD, Nancy Dassoff, PhD, Ira Levin, PhD, Janice Schreckengost, MA, AB, Stephen P. Stelzner,
PhD, and B. Eileen Altman, PhD* (Vol. 6, No. 1, 1989). *"An invaluable compendium for the
prevention practitioner, as well as the researcher, laying out the essentials for developing effective prevention programs in the community. . . . This is a book which should be in the prevention
practitioner's library, to read, re-read, and ponder." (The Community Psychologist)*

**Prevention: Toward a Multidisciplinary Approach,** edited by Leonard A. Jason, PhD, Robert D.
Felner, PhD, John N. Moritsugu, PhD, and Robert E. Hess, PhD* (Vol. 5, No. 2, 1987). *"Will
not only be of intellectual value to the professional but also to students in courses aimed at presenting a refreshingly comprehensive picture of the conceptual and practical relationships between community and prevention." (Seymour B. Sarason, Associate Professor of Psychology,
Yale University)*

**Prevention and Health: Directions for Policy and Practice,** edited by Alfred H. Katz, PhD, Jared A.
Hermalin, PhD, and Robert E. Hess, PhD* (Vol. 5, No. 1, 1987). *Read about the most current efforts being undertaken to promote better health.*

**The Ecology of Prevention: Illustrating Mental Health Consultation,** edited by James G. Kelly,
PhD, and Robert E. Hess, PhD* (Vol. 4, No 3/4, 1987). *"Will provide the consultant with a very
useful framework and the student with an appreciation for the time and commitment necessary to
bring about lasting changes of a preventive nature." (The Community Psychologist)*

**Beyond the Individual: Environmental Approaches and Prevention,** edited by Abraham
Wandersman, PhD, and Robert E. Hess, PhD* (Vol. 4, No. 1/2, 1985). *"This excellent book has
immediate appeal for those involved with environmental psychology . . . likely to be of great interest to those working in the areas of community psychology, planning, and design." (Austra-
lian Journal of Psychology)*

**Prevention: The Michigan Experience,** edited by Betty Tableman, MPA, and Robert E. Hess, PhD*
(Vol. 3, No. 4, 1985). *An in-depth look at one state's outstanding prevention programs.*

**Studies in Empowerment: Steps Toward Understanding and Action,** edited by Julian Rappaport,
Carolyn Swift, and Robert E. Hess, PhD* (Vol. 3, No. 2/3, 1984). *"Provides diverse applications
of the empowerment model to the promotion of mental health and the prevention of mental illness." (Prevention Forum Newsline)*

**Aging and Prevention: New Approaches for Preventing Health and Mental Health Problems in
Older Adults,** edited by Sharon P. Simson, Laura Wilson, Jared Hermalin, PhD, and Robert E.
Hess, PhD* (Vol. 3, No. 1, 1983). *"Highly recommended for professionals and laymen interested in modern viewpoints and techniques for avoiding many physical and mental health problems of the elderly. Written by highly qualified contributors with extensive experience in their
respective fields." (The Clinical Gerontologist)*

**Strategies for Needs Assessment in Prevention,** edited by Alex Zautra, Kenneth Bachrach, and Robert E. Hess, PhD* (Vol. 2, No. 4, 1983). *"An excellent survey on applied techniques for doing
needs assessments. . . . It should be on the shelf of anyone involved in prevention." (Journal of
Pediatric Psychology)*

**Innovations in Prevention,** edited by Robert E. Hess, PhD, and Jared Hermalin, PhD* (Vol. 2, No.
3, 1983). *An exciting book that provides invaluable insights on effective prevention programs.*

**Rx Television: Enhancing the Preventive Impact of TV,** edited by Joyce Sprafkin, Carolyn Swift,
PhD, and Robert E. Hess, PhD* (Vol. 2, No. 1/2, 1983). *"The successful interventions reported
in this volume make interesting reading on two grounds. First, they show quite clearly how powerful television can be in molding children. Second, they illustrate how this power can be used
for good ends." (Contemporary Psychology)*

***Early Intervention Programs for Infants,*** edited by Howard A. Moss, MD, Robert E. Hess, PhD, and Carolyn Swift, PhD* (Vol. 1, No. 4, 1982). *"A useful resource book for those child psychiatrists, paediatricians, and psychologists interested in early intervention and prevention." (The Royal College of Psychiatrists)*

***Helping People to Help Themselves: Self-Help and Prevention,*** edited by Leonard D. Borman, PhD, Leslie E. Borck, PhD, Robert E. Hess, PhD, and Frank L. Pasquale* (Vol. 1, No. 3, 1982). *"A timely volume . . . a mine of information for interested clinicians, and should stimulate those wishing to do systematic research in the self-help area." (The Journal of Nervous and Mental Disease)*

***Evaluation and Prevention in Human Services,*** edited by Jared Hermalin, PhD, and Jonathan A. Morell, PhD* (Vol. 1, No. 1/2, 1982). *Features methods and problems related to the evaluation of prevention programs.*

# Culture, Peers, and Delinquency

Clifford R. O'Donnell
Editor

*Culture, Peers, and Delinquency* has been co-published simultaneously as *Journal of Prevention & Intervention in the Community*, Volume 25, Number 2 2003.

The Haworth Press, Inc.

New York • London • Victoria (AU)
**www.HaworthPress.com**

*Culture, Peers, and Delinquency* has been co-published simultaneously as *Journal of Prevention & Intervention in the Community*™, Volume 25, Number 2 2003.

The development, preparation, and publication of this work has been undertaken with great care. However, the publisher, employees, editors, and agents of The Haworth Press and all imprints of The Haworth Press, Inc., including The Haworth Medical Press® and Pharmaceutical Products Press®, are not responsible for any errors contained herein or for consequences that may ensue from use of materials or information contained in this work. Opinions expressed by the author(s) are not necessarily those of The Haworth Press, Inc. With regard to case studies, identities and circumstances of individuals discussed herein have been changed to protect confidentiality. Any resemblance to actual persons, living or dead, is entirely coincidental.

The Haworth Press, Inc., 10 Alice Street, Binghamton, NY 13904-1580 USA

Cover design by Lora Wiggins

**Library of Congress Cataloging-in-Publication Data**

Culture, peers, and delinquency / edited by Clifford R. O'Donnell
        p. cm.
"Co-published simultaneously as the Journal of Prevention & Intervention in the Community, Volume 25, Number 2 2003."
    ISBN 0-7890-2138-2 (hard cover : alk. paper) – ISBN 0-7890-2139-0 (soft cover : alk. paper)
1. Juvenile delinquency. 2. Peer pressure. 3. Juvenile delinquency–Prevention. I. O'Donnell, Clifford R. II. Journal of prevention & intervention in the community.
    HV9069.C85 2003
    364.36–dc21

                                                            2003005331

# Indexing, Abstracting & Website/Internet Coverage

This section provides you with a list of major indexing & abstracting services. That is to say, each service began covering this periodical during the year noted in the right column. Most Websites which are listed below have indicated that they will either post, disseminate, compile, archive, cite or alert their own Website users with research-based content from this work. (This list is as current as the copyright date of this publication.)

Abstracting, Website/Indexing Coverage . . . . . . . . . Year When Coverage Began

- *Behavioral Medicine Abstracts* . . . . . . . . . . . . . . . . . . . . . . . . . . . . . **1996**

- *CNPIEC Reference Guide: Chinese National Directory of Foreign Periodicals* . . . . . . . . . . . . . . . . . . . . . . . . . . . . . . . . **1996**

- *Educational Research Abstracts (ERA) (online database)* *<www.tandf.co.uk/era>* . . . . . . . . . . . . . . . . . . . . . . . . . . . . . **2002**

- *EMBASE/Excerpta Medica Secondary Publishing Division <www.elsevier.nl>* . . . . . . . . . . . . . . . . . . . . . . . . . . . . **1996**

- *e-psyche, LLC <www.e-psyche.net>* . . . . . . . . . . . . . . . . . . . . . . . . **2001**

- *Family & Society Studies Worldwide <www.nisc.com>* . . . . . . . . . . . **1996**

- *Gay & Lesbian Abstracts <www.nisc.com>* . . . . . . . . . . . . . . . . . . . . **2000**

(continued)

(continued)

*Special Bibliographic Notes related to special journal issues
(separates) and indexing/abstracting:*

- indexing/abstracting services in this list will also cover material in any "separate" that is co-published simultaneously with Haworth's special thematic journal issue or DocuSerial. Indexing/abstracting usually covers material at the article/chapter level.
- monographic co-editions are intended for either non-subscribers or libraries which intend to purchase a second copy for their circulating collections.
- monographic co-editions are reported to all jobbers/wholesalers/approval plans. The source journal is listed as the "series" to assist the prevention of duplicate purchasing in the same manner utilized for books-in-series.
- to facilitate user/access services all indexing/abstracting services are encouraged to utilize the co-indexing entry note indicated at the bottom of the first page of each article/chapter/contribution.
- this is intended to assist a library user of any reference tool (whether print, electronic, online, or CD-ROM) to locate the monographic version if the library has purchased this version but not a subscription to the source journal.
- individual articles/chapters in any Haworth publication are also available through the Haworth Document Delivery Service (HDDS).

# ABOUT THE EDITOR

**Clifford R. O'Donnell, PhD,** is Professor of Psychology and Director of the Community and Culture Graduate Program at the University of Hawaii. Dr. O'Donnell was awarded Fellow status in the Society for Community Research and Action (APA Division 27) "in recognition of his outstanding contributions to the field of community research and action." He also received an "Outstanding Professor" award from the University of Hawaii Psi Chi as well as awards from the Melissa Institute for the Prevention and Treatment of Violence and from the Council of Program Directors in Community Research and Action.

Dr. O'Donnell is a Scientific Board Member of the Melissa Institute for the Prevention and Treatment of Violence. He has served as Chair of the Council of Program Directors in Community Research and Action, as Director of the Center for Youth Research at the University, and as an Executive Board Member of the Consortium for Children, Families, and the Law. He has published extensively on such topics as delinquency prevention, school violence, firearm deaths among children and youth, social networks, programs for at-risk youth, community intervention, culturally compatible forms of community development, and education and employment in community psychology.

Dr. O'Donnell has provided consultation to the United States Peace Corps in Micronesia, the Zuni Native American Tribe in New Mexico, and delinquency programs across the United States. He has provided program evaluation services to schools, correctional facilities, courts, settlement house programs, drug treatment programs, and Head Start in Hawaii. He has served on the Evaluation Advisory Panel of the Navajo Early Intervention Project, on the Evaluation Resource Team of the Hawaii Community Services Council, and on the Hawaii Juvenile Justice Interagency Board. He has presented invited testimony to the United States Congress as well as briefings on subjects that include the U.N. Convention on the Rights of Children, minority overrepresentation in the justice system, methods of reducing firearm injuries and deaths, the relationship of child maltreatment to delinquency and violence, and the overrepresentation of youth with disabilities in the juvenile justice system.

# Culture, Peers, and Delinquency

## CONTENTS

# Introduction:
# Juvenile Delinquency:
# Culture and Community,
# Person and Society, Theory and Research

Roland G. Tharp

*University of California, Santa Cruz*

**SUMMARY.** Studies of juvenile delinquency that incorporate concepts of culture, community, social organization, socialization and gender are rare. This collection of such papers, each concerned with delinquency in the several cultures of Japan and Hawaii, examines the interplay of historical, traditional culture with contemporary youth culture, the relationship between individual outcome and community disorganization, and peer relationships conditioned by gender. These complexities are discussed in the light of the community-peer model (that delinquency de-

Roland G. Tharp won the Grawemeyer Award in 1993 for the book *Rousing Minds to Life*, based on twenty years' work as Principal Investigator of the Kamehameha Early Education Program (KEEP). He is Professor Emeritus at the Universities of Hawaii and California, and has also taught at Arizona and Stanford. His research and theory in the fields of psychotherapy, behavior therapy, family relationships, human development, education, culture, and linguistic diversity span 40 years and 250 publications. He is Director of the federal government's National Center for Research on Education, Diversity & Excellence (CREDE).

Address correspondence to: Roland G. Tharp, 307 Dickens Way, Santa Cruz, CA 95064.

[Haworth co-indexing entry note]: "Introduction: Juvenile Delinquency: Culture and Community, Person and Society, Theory and Research." Tharp, Roland G. Co-published simultaneously in *Journal of Prevention & Intervention in the Community* (The Haworth Press, Inc.) Vol. 25, No. 2, 2003, pp. 1-11; and: *Culture, Peers, and Delinquency* (ed: Clifford R. O'Donnell) The Haworth Press, Inc., 2003, pp. 1-11. Single or multiple copies of this article are available for a fee from The Haworth Document Delivery Service [1-800-HAWORTH, 9:00 a.m. - 5:00 p.m. (EST). E-mail address: docdelivery@haworthpress.com].

velops through activity with similar peers, in settings lacking adult supervision) (O'Donnell, this volume), and in terms of cultural-historical-activity theory, an approach that enables integration of those concepts into an understanding of the etiology, prevention and treatment of delinquency. *[Article copies available for a fee from The Haworth Document Delivery Service: 1-800-HAWORTH. E-mail address: <docdelivery@haworthpress. com> Website: <http://www.HaworthPress.com> © 2003 by The Haworth Press, Inc. All rights reserved.]*

**KEYWORDS.** Delinquency, culture, community, peers, gender, activity settings

Juvenile delinquency has been studied by every major social science discipline–psychology, sociology, anthropology, criminology, education, community studies–with emphases on family, schools, culture, communities, corrections, identity and alienation, and group dynamics. The five papers gathered here are particularly ambitious. They seek variously to integrate and rationalize the relationships among these concepts, testing their ideas against current hypotheses, in attempts to better understand the development of delinquency and the best approaches to its treatment.

This undertaking is timely, because it is now feasible–due to the development of cultural-historical-activity theory, an approach that by its nature integrates and rationalizes the dynamics among these concepts.

## *CULTURAL-HISTORICAL-ACTIVITY THEORY*

Cultural-historical-activity theory (CHAT) is centrally concerned with issues of culture, language, cognition, community and socialization. In brief, CHAT holds that *primary socialization of infants and young children (and indeed, all later socialization into new communities of practice) is accomplished through joint, meaningful activity with guidance by more accomplished participants, principally through language exchanges* or other semiotic processes (O'Donnell & Tharp, 1990; Tharp & Gallimore, 1989; Vygotsky, 1978, 1981; Wells & Claxton, 2002). Language vocabularies and routines acquired by the learners through these processes are the elements that account for community, linguistic and cultural continuity. They are also the primary cognitive tools for individual and group problem-solving and adaptation. Attitudes and values are similarly and simultaneously formed through those linguistic and paralinguistic exchanges. Since, in this theory, *activity* (particularly joint activity) is the nexus in which language and cognition are developed, it follows that patterns of activity have a cultural basis, and also that through activity, culture develops and changes. The developmental history of the community is encoded in its culture, and so the community's history exists into present time, a still potent element of current experience.

Thus, culture is that mass of representations, symbols, statements and text, shared activities, values, and attitudes that have accumulated historically in the community. To some degree, the definitions of community and culture are circular, since the community, as it shares practices and activities, accumulates culture and perpetuates it, by engaging in joint activity with new members and interpreting themselves during it.

Few humans are members of only one community of practice, of one culture. A typical subject of study in the papers below might have simultaneous membership in the communities and cultures that make him or her Asian, Vietnamese, Vietnamese-American immigrant, local Hawaiian, Global Youth, high schooler, male or female, or delinquent.

The processes for socialization into these communities are acculturative, and they are dynamically equivalent for each. That is, for each group, membership is achieved by joint activity with more senior members, who interpret the activity in terms of the symbols (predominantly verbal) that establish the meaning and value of the community association. This is equally true for 'delinquency' as for 'Vietnamese,' though the senior members who accomplish the association are in the one case parents and elders, and in the other, more experienced gang members. In all cases, the vehicle for the process is *joint activity*.

Every individual is to some extent multicultural, as we are all members of multiple communities of practice. These memberships are simultaneous, and the corresponding sets of values and action probabilities are held simultaneously in repertoire, brought into action by the community-of-context in which activity occurs. A youth of Japan is no less Japanese when delinquent, though many 'Japanese' cultural values may be deeply suppressed by activity preferences that are driven by the more contextually powerful delinquent gang community. Disentangling the cultural/community sources of specific elements of delinquent activity is a complex task, and worth the effort, not only for the intellectual satisfaction of understanding, but for guidance in the design of appropriate corrective intervention. Good examples of this complex work will be seen in these papers, to which we should now turn, to test the utility of the theory against their data.

How important are their cultural identifications in understanding delinquent youth in a multicultural city? Joie Acosta's data suggest that there are some intercultural differences in major descriptors of the attitudes and activities of youth in Honolulu. However, these differences are less impressive than the similarities. The Caucasian cultural group appears to represent the central tendency of the overall sample, not differing from any other cultural group on the five factor scores, though the East Asian, South-East Asian and Polynesian groups differ from one another in the three factors of social interaction, language opportunities, and cultural activities. None of the four groups differed from one another in peer attachment or peer influence. The author glosses these data as supportive of the existence of a general youth culture. While adolescents do not abandon the cultures of their ethnicity, community and families, they are much alike in peer relationships, regardless of cultural differences.

In any event, the data on cultural dimensions do not map comfortably onto the four geo-cultural groups. For example, cultural identification was highest for Polynesian/Micronesian, and lowest for South-East Asians–yet these two are overrepresented in group arrest rates. However, when rates of participation in types of activities are examined, arrest rates are correlated with group differences in reading, unsupervised partying, and concert attendance. The author argues that these activities are often the basis for the formation of peer groups. Thus, the general conclusion emerges–cultural variables, as commonly understood, are less predictive of delinquency than are features of the general youth culture. This culture, toward which subgroups are adapting, is representative of the putative 'Western' value for adolescent independence. (Thus, in the explanatory circle, culture reappears, as a dominant centripetal force for acculturation.)

Acosta also argues for the pertinence of the agreement of her data with the propositions of activity theory, and regrets the lack of delinquency interventions based on peer group relationships and activities.

There is much in this article that is supportive of, and, indeed, illuminating for CHAT. For users of this approach, culture and activity are mutually constitutive. In Acosta's account, the dynamics of cultural evolution include the activities around which youth from many cultures gather. Such accounts must also carefully examine the patterns of activity within intersecting cultures. Acosta does so, in her attribution of 'independence' to the dominant Western culture, and then asserts that other cultural groups are moving closer to that pattern through, presumably, association in activity. This 'independence' is presumed to be correlated with, if not determinative of, unsupervised group adolescent activities, which are themselves associated with arrest rates.

Two issues of fact arise in this analysis. First, is it a value of Western culture that *adolescents* be independent, or that adolescents are to be gradually weaned toward the independence of adulthood? This difference is consequential for the design of interventions, because another point of intersection that community interventionists must consider is that between the adolescent's community culture and the general youth culture. Both the practicality of and the responses to such interventions will be affected by the congruence, or lack of it, between the two. For example, age-graded social organization is a well-known, and well-neigh definitive characteristic of Polynesian societies (Boggs, 1985; D'Amato, 1987, 1988; Gallimore, Boggs & Jordan, 1974). Young Hawaiian children are expected to organize themselves as sibling and/or like-age groups, which are to be maximally self-supervising. These groups can expect supervision at times when their own group independence breaks down, and they are likely to regret it. The supervising adolescents, meanwhile, have a parallel relationship to adults, who also intervene with the youth group only when problems appear. In this instance, independence *of* adolescents is a persistent and potent cultural value. Trying to 'correct' this pattern of adult-adolescent interaction is sure to encounter culturally-based stiff resistance from all parties.

## DELINQUENT ACTIVITY, CULTURE, AND COMMUNITY

The relationship of delinquent activity to patterns observably normative in the host culture is complex, but not mysterious. I recall that idea dawning on me–at dawn in Las Vegas, after a long night with my hosts in a delinquency-prevention consultation visit. The most frequent early-delinquency offense for Las Vegas youth was–curfew violations. (This in a city inexhaustible in its determination to keep adults up and gambling all night [Tharp & Wetzel, 1969].) Most delinquent and delinquency-supportive activities are rooted in, present in, and for adults, stimulated by cultural and economic community decisions. For example, delinquent tendencies are associated with 'hanging out in the mall' in Acosta's Honolulu study. That association would be unlikely in a traditional community's market, where adolescents are in close proximity to family and adult members of their own neighborhood community members. Separating market from community is economical and convenient for Honolulu adults, who do not seem to resist spending time wandering the malls themselves, at least long enough to get the shopping and eating done. But a byproduct of the isolation of the market is the distancing of appropriate supervising adults from idling youth groups.

Much delinquency can be seen as a youthful lack of self-control over behaviors clearly discernable, more modulated, but often normative, in the adult culture, and which are inadvertently supported by patterns of adult-youth interaction and activity that are congruent with cultural values.

Both of these features are richly illustrated in Yuko Yamamiya's study of juvenile delinquency and policing in Japan. Her palette of demographics, economics, history and cultural analysis sketches a picture of increasing Japanese delinquency, appalling to the reader and frightening to Japanese adulthood. Most useful is her identification of Japanese cultural concepts that are implicated, violated, distorted (but clearly and deeply involved) in juvenile delinquent activity. Like Acosta's Honolulu, youth in Japan–for all their homogeneous cultural history and identification–engage in joint activity in bands; find group solidarity, support and meaning in their peer associations; and are alienated from adults of the home and school. Yamamiya, like Acosta, implicates the corruption of Japanese collectivism by Western individualism, though I find it no more convincing. As with Polynesian delinquents, and with even more fervor, Japanese delinquent youth find their collectivist cultural valuation of authority, subservience and obligation satisfied in power-stratified gangs. Yamamiya's descriptions suggest not a weakening or failure of traditional Japanese psychocultural values, but youth groups that have found satisfactions for those values greater than in the homes and schools from which they were alienated and rebellious. Current delinquency is continuous with the developmental patterns characteristic of recruits to the yakuza–where these same traditional psychocultural needs continue to be met.

As for the specific actions of developing Japanese delinquency, youth society is 'saturated with violence, often with erotic overtones,' and it values explosive rage. In these descriptions, Yamamiya is clear, useful and graphic, reporting, for example, that 50% of junior high school students read pornographic books. As an occasional traveler on the Tokyo-Kyoto trains, I notice that so do their fathers. In her analysis, Yamamiya does not discuss the traditional Japanese cultural elements of rage, violence and Eros. In the restraints of poetry, pottery, tea, music and dance, the sublime calm and patience of the self-disciplined and obedient Japanese is among the most admired of world images. Yet that image is foregrounded against an explosive potential of rage and cruelty that consistently erupts in Japanese film, drama and entertainments of the demimonde, providing the stuff of tragedy, as in Mushima–but also with criminal ferocity in such settings as Nanking and World War II prisoner camps. A full understanding of the contents of Japanese delinquency will require considering this tension between the potential for violence and its social and personal control. As Yamamiya says, Japan's traditional cultural values are pointed toward the social control of delinquency, through regulation of social relationships. Though out of control in Japanese delinquents, these emotional elements are hardly unfamiliar to traditional society; what is alien is their inappropriate and unmodulated expression. Traditional supervision and socialization activities that have heretofore been adequate to the gradual transition to adult self-control and balance are becoming unreliable.

The world's marginal youth–disappointed, frustrated, rejected, angered by school and home–are like the mine canaries in the new globalization of transportation, communication, commerce and migration. Their symptoms alert us to the breakdown and toxicity when traditional cultures lose effective conditions for supervising youth into the self-control necessary for cultural socialization. Youth are most likely to go bad in the ways their culture has always feared, has always supervised against, has always banded together to assist themselves to resist. Youth go bad in the ways of their own cultures, but–like good canaries–show us poison in the air, long before we notice that somewhere, something below the surface of culture is ruptured.

These fissures, developing in the activity patterns shared by maturing youth and their adult supervisors, can be due to language differences, cultural distances between generations expanded by schools, lack of time of hard-working immigrant families, or many other local conditions. Are these community problems the *cause* of delinquency? They are certainly contributive, but the causative chain is more complex.

Is it possible that in rapidly modernizing traditional societies, or those of immigrated communities, the ruptures of adult supervision and socialization increase the relative influence of peers? I suspect that a normal shift toward peer orientation is phylogenetically prepared as part of the differentiation of maturing youth from their families of origin. However, in conditions of lessening familial and community activity participation with youth, peer associations and activities tend to fill the relationship and support needs. Thus, the activities of the peer group–delinquent or non-delinquent–into which an adolescent moves will be the most potent and the proximal determinant of his or her own development.

This pattern is visible in Nghi Dong Thai's study of Vietnamese youth gangs in Honolulu. Adults consistently blame community disorganization and lack of parental supervision, communication and support for their youth's gang activities. They are not wrong, certainly, but they do not recognize the proximal cause, which is peer influences. Youth themselves attribute influence exclusively to peers, and they are correct, though they do not see that peers are the more crucial when adult supervision is shrunken. An illuminating aspect of this study is similar dynamic for those Vietnamese youth who become delinquent and those who do not. Peer influences are central for both, and association with delinquent peers is determinative for youth, whether or not they are alienated from their families and school. They, like youth-in-school everywhere, are more likely to encounter delinquent peers if they themselves are failing in school, have infrequent activity with their community adults, or are excluded and harassed by school associates. But not all alienated youth are driven into association with delinquent peers, and if they are not, they do not become delinquent themselves.

This dynamic has been developed into a clear theoretical hypothesis by O'Donnell (1998, 2000), who analyzes homes, schools and neighborhoods in terms of the dysfunctions that increase the likelihood that their youth will spend time with similar peers, in settings lacking adult supervision. O'Donnell's propositions are, in my judgement, persuasive, consistent with the available data, buttressed by solid theory, and testable by alterations in treatment designs.

However, before declaring that this view has swept the table, we must attend to the gender-difference studies reviewed and expanded here by Renee Galbavy. The mixed-culture incarcerated adolescents interviewed in Hawaii by Galbavy differed sharply by gender, in their attributions of cause for their delinquency. Males (mean age 17.5) state that they are under heavy influence from their male peers whom they wish to impress. Females (mean age 15.3) blame themselves and their families for their misdeeds. In general, the stories of the males correspond well to the community-peer model–school failure, gravitation to delinquent peers, peer solidarity, mutual influence, and shared delinquent activity (O'Donnell, 1998, 2000). Females were more likely to run away from their dysfunctional families, into delinquent activities with others, certainly, but less to please peers than as impulsive, self-directed participation.

An important feature of this study is the delinquents' uniform positive valuation of the detention facility school. The males, at least, had little good to say for the schools they avoided before incarceration. But the activity of school takes on different (positive) meaning in the context of the incarcerated community. Activity is always interpreted by the joint participants, including educators with authority and resources to dispense.

Galbavy acknowledges the small *n* of her research, the age difference between the gender groups, and that she interviewed only youth already incarcerated (a relatively small proportion of Hawaii offenders). Whether or not the specifics of her findings are found to be generalizable, future research in this entire field must look more carefully at gender differences, and attend to her call for treating males and females as separate populations for prevention, treatment and research. Her findings for females are not inconsistent with the basic O'Donnell explanatory framework, but if the gender-specific dynamics are verified by further research, they are consequential for treatment design.

## IMPLICATIONS FOR PREVENTION AND TREATMENT

In the light of the theory and data presented here, prevention of delinquency might be best directed toward those conditions more distal in the causal chain–toward improving opportunities for family and other adults to engage in activities with adolescents during which supervision/socialization can occur. Such prevention programs would reduce the attraction to, frequency of exposure to, and involvement in activity with already-delinquent peers. These efforts might range from family counseling to organization of community-agency programs of youth activity in which adults are co-participants–the best role for supervision.

School alienation is a specific risk factor for delinquency, particularly salient in recent immigrant groups. CHAT provides both explanation and guidance for how this risk might be reduced, as in efforts to reform schooling through increasing cultural compatibility (Tharp & Gallimore, 1989). This argument states that culturally-based secondary socialization processes (schooling; incorporation into communities of practice) can be facilitated by activating the learners' cognitive and linguistic tools laid down by earlier primary socialization. Since activity (particularly joint activity) is the nexus in which language and cognition are developed, it follows that patterns of activity have a cultural basis.

Thus, competence in various forms of activity required by school deter-mines the degree and quality of participation in school activity. Positive learning outcomes are increased when school participation structures are congruent with those in the learners' repertoires. Such features as turn-taking, wait-time, observational learning vs. trial-and-error, and various courtesies and conventions of conversation have characteristic features in each culture, and they differ from the conventions of schools of the common tradition. Interventions for school that radically increase joint activity among teachers and peers (resulting in increases in pro-so-cial inclusion) have been described and evaluated by Tharp, Estrada, Dalton, and Yamauchi (2000).

Treatment programs for youth already involved in delinquent activ-ity, by all accounts here, should focus on altering the composition, the patterns of association and the activities of peer groups. Although the-ory and evidence overwhelmingly point to this as the appropriate locus for attention, vexing issues in program design remain. For example, Nghi Dong Thai suggests that school and police authorities should not force association of new offenders with delinquent peers, by gathering them all into punitive settings and activities. She suggests that an iso-lated, or pro-social group-affiliated activity of public service is far more rational. Even this simple, persuasive policy suggestion quickly gets complex. In what proportion can these first offenders be absorbed into pro-social groups? Peer influence flows in every direction. Mixed groups of delinquents and their non-delinquent 'buddies' tend to alter their values toward the mean, as in the classic O'Donnell, Lydgate, and Fo (1979) study. What proportion, conditioned by which cultural, age, or gender variables, provide good odds for good social outcome?

At the other extreme is treatment of incarcerated groups, whose peer composition is necessarily homogeneous. Hopes for pro-social devel-opment lie with the authority of adults introduced into that community. Here theory does give guidance, suggesting that joint activity among the delinquents and supervising adults should be maximized if pro-so-cial attitudinal development is to occur (such as the shift toward posi-tive valuation of school).

Each of the papers below discusses treatment alternatives and out-comes, in the light of our available data and theory. Their introduction of the complexities of culture and community, family and school into the study of delinquency has clarified the work still to be done.

# REFERENCES

Acosta, J. (2003). The effects of cultural differences on peer group relationships. In O'Donnell, C. R. (Ed.), *Culture, peers, and delinquency.* Binghamton, NY: The Haworth Press, Inc.

Boggs, S. T. (1985). *Speaking, relating and learning: A study of Hawaiian children at home and at school.* New York: Ablex Publishing.

D'Amato, J. (1987). The belly of the beast: On cultural differences, castelike status, and the politics of school. *Anthropology and Education Quarterly, 18*(4), 357-360.

D'Amato, J. (1988). "Acting": Hawaiian children's resistance to teachers. *The Elementary School Journal, 88*(5), 529-544.

Galbavy, R. J. (2003). Juvenile delinquency: Peer influences, gender differences and prevention. In O'Donnell, C. R. (Ed.), *Culture, peers, and delinquency.* Binghamton, NY: The Haworth Press, Inc.

Gallimore, R., Boggs, J. W., & Jordan, C. (1974). *Culture, behavior and education: A study of Hawaiian-Americans.* Beverly Hills, CA: Sage Publications.

O'Donnell, C. R. (1998, May). *Peers and delinquency: Implications for prevention and intervention.* Presentation at the Violence and Youth: Overcoming the Odds: Helping Children and Families at Risk Conference, Miami, FL.

O'Donnell, C. R. (2000). *Youth with disabilities in the juvenile justice system: A literature review.* Clemson, SC: Consortium on Children, Families, and the Law, Clemson University, Institute on Family and Neighborhood Life.

O'Donnell, C. R. (2003). Culture, peers, and delinquency: Implications for the community-peer model of delinquency. In O'Donnell, C. R. (Ed.), *Culture, peers, and delinquency.* Binghamton, NY: The Haworth Press, Inc.

O'Donnell, C. R., Lydgate, T., & Fo, W. S. O. (1979). The buddy system: Review and follow-up. *Child Behavior Therapy, 1,* 161-169.

O'Donnell, C. R. & Tharp, R. G. (1990). Community intervention guided by theoretical development. In Bellack, A. S., Hersen, M., & Kazdin, A. E. (Eds.), *International handbook of behavior modification and therapy,* 2nd Ed. (pp. 251-266). New York: Plenum Press.

Thai, N. D. (2003). Vietnamese youth gangs in Honolulu. In O'Donnell, C. R. (Ed.), *Culture, peers, and delinquency.* Binghamton, NY: The Haworth Press, Inc.

Tharp, R. G., Estrada, P., Dalton, S. S., & Yamauchi, L.A. (2000). *Teaching transformed: Achieving excellence, fairness, inclusion and harmony.* Boulder, CO: Westview Press.

Tharp, R. G. & Gallimore, R. (1989). *Rousing minds to life.* Cambridge: Cambridge University Press.

Tharp, R. G. & Wetzel, R. J. (1969). *Behavior modification in the natural environment.* New York: Academic Press.

Vygotsky, L.S. (1981). The genesis of higher mental functions. In J. V. Wertsch (Ed.), *The concept of activity in Soviet psychology.* Amonk, NY: M. E. Sharpe.

Vygotsky, L. S. (1978). *Mind in society: The development of higher psychological processes.* (M. Cole, V. John-Steiner, S. Scribner, & E. Souberman, Eds. & Trans.) Cambridge, MA: Harvard University Press.

Wells, G. & Claxton, G. (2002). (Eds.) *Learning for life in the 21st century.* Oxford, UK: Blackwell Publishing.

Yamamiya, Y. (2003). Juvenile delinquency in Japan. In O'Donnell, C. R. (Ed.), *Culture, peers, and delinquency.* Binghamton, NY: The Haworth Press, Inc.

# The Effects of Cultural Differences on Peer Group Relationships

Joie Acosta

*University of Hawaii at Manoa*

**SUMMARY.** The goal of this study was to explore delinquency as an interdependent relationship between the social context and the individual or group of individuals being studied and to gain insight into the relationship between culture, peer group relationships, and delinquency. The results suggested that certain types of activities are more closely linked with delinquent behavior, rather than specific aspects of peer group relations. Cultural group differences were not manifested in peer group relationships. Therefore, these findings suggest the importance of youth culture rather than traditional culture as a protective or degenerative factor in delinquent behavior. Further research on the role of youth culture

---

Joie Acosta is a PhD candidate in the Community and Cultural Psychology program at the University of Hawaii at Manoa and has a specilized certificate in Disaster Management, Humanitarian Assistance and International Peacekeeping. She coordinates a State Incentive Grant evaluating substance abuse prevention programs for adolescent youth in Hawaii. She serves as a student reviewer for the *American Journal of Community Psychology* and was recently awarded a grant from the Melissa Institute for Violence Prevention and Treatment to conduct her dissertation research on chronic community violence.

Address correspondence to : Joie Acosta, Department of Psychology, 2430 Campus Road, University of Hawaii at Manoa, Honolulu, HI 96822-2216.

[Haworth co-indexing entry note]: "The Effects of Cultural Differences on Peer Group Relationships." Acosta, Joie. Co-published simultaneously in *Journal of Prevention & Intervention in the Community* (The Haworth Press, Inc.) Vol. 25, No. 2, 2003, pp. 13-26; and: *Culture, Peers, and Delinquency* (ed: Clifford R. O'Donnell) The Haworth Press, Inc., 2003, pp. 13-26. Single or multiple copies of this article are available for a fee from The Haworth Document Delivery Service [1-800-HAWORTH, 9:00 a.m. - 5:00 p.m. (EST). E-mail address: docdelivery@haworthpress.com].

10.1300/J005v25n02_02

and peer groups in delinquent behavior is needed because of the theoretical and practical implications for prevention and intervention programs. *[Article copies available for a fee from The Haworth Document Delivery Service: 1-800-HAWORTH. E-mail address: <docdelivery@haworthpress.com> Website: <http://www.HaworthPress.com> © 2003 by The Haworth Press, Inc. All rights reserved.]*

**KEYWORDS.** Delinquency, culture, peers, community

In the United States in 1999, juveniles were involved in one out of every six arrests made by law enforcement officers (17%), one out of every six arrests for violent crime (16%) and one out of every three arrests for property crime (32%) (Snyder, 1999). In 1999, juvenile violent crime arrests have declined 36% from their peak in 1994, while the number of juveniles arrested for drug abuse violations has increased 132% (Snyder, 1999)!

Juvenile delinquency is a phenomena that is affected by a myriad of variables (Adler & Laufer, 1995; Agnew, 1993; Beccaria, 1974; Booth & Osgood, 1993; Bursik, 1988; Carey, 1992; Cloninger & Gottesman, 1987; Gardner & Shoemaker, 1994; Horwitz & Wasserman, 1980; Lyerly & Skipper, 1981; McCarthy & Smith, 1986; Mednick, Gabrielli, & Hutchings, 1987; Ray & Downs, 1986; Sampson, 1994; Tanioka & Glaser, 1991; Thomas & Bishop, 1984; Wells, 1991). Among these variables, peer associations have a particularly significant influence on adolescent delinquency. Delinquent behavior occurs most often in a group setting (Emler, Reicher, & Ross, 1987) and deviant peer associations can perpetuate delinquent behavior through peer pressure, modeling, and social reinforcement (Coie, Terry, Zakriski, & Lochman, 1995; Dishion, McCord, & Poulin, 1999). Research has suggested that one of the foremost predictors of delinquent behavior is engaging in a social context with deviant peers (Arnold & Hughes, 1999; O'Donnell, Manos, & Chesney-Lind, 1987; White, Pandina, & LaGrange, 1987).

An in-depth inquiry into the cultural variations of adolescence indicated that adolescent development is significantly effected by culture (Schlegel & Barry, 1991). Cultural differences are considered a key contextual variable in adolescent development (Friedman, 1993). Therefore, culture can have a protective or degenerative effect on adolescent development and needs to be considered in any investigation of adolescent behavior. Cultural beliefs and values are mediated through the family, school, neighborhood and, most importantly for delinquency, the peer group. Therefore, it may be important to include cultural differences in models of juvenile delinquency.

Although research on the role of cultural differences in other areas, such as emotional development (Banerjee, 1997), is prominent, there has been considerably less research on the effects of cultural differences on the peer-delinquency relationship. Recent research has explored the link between both Chinese and Mexican acculturation and delinquency. A study of Chinese-Canadians linked coherence to traditional Chinese culture with decreased rates of delinquency (Wong, 1999). Research on Latino adolescents has also indicated that there is a significant positive relationship between acculturation and delinquent behavior (Vega, Khoury, Zimmerman, Gil, & Warheit, 1995; Wall, Power, & Arbona, 1993). These studies suggest that acculturation increases the risk of delinquent behavior.

A possible explanation of this acculturation-delinquency effect is that acculturated youth are integrated into a youth culture that directly affects adolescent behavior. Indeed, throughout the industrialized world a youth culture has emerged which is qualitatively different from and often stands in opposition to traditional cultures. This youth culture establishes different norms for adolescents. Consequently, a new set of values, addressing age-related concerns, perceptions, and behaviors, is established, and a group identity that is the basis for the youth culture is formed (Corsaro, 1985).

The purpose of this study is to assess the effects of cultural differences on peer relationships and group delinquency rates. American youth with different ethnic/racial cultural roots are compared to see if their different traditional cultural roots affect their peer relationships or if these relationships are sufficiently similar to be considered within a common youth culture.

## *METHOD*

### *Participants*

A total of 101 students were recruited from an urban high school in Honolulu. Of these, 9 participated in a focus group, 5 were interviewed individually, and 86 completed a questionnaire. The focus group and the individual interviews provided the opportunity for the students to discuss culture and peer relationships. The information obtained from this process was then used in sections of the questionnaire.

The focus group consisted of seven females and two males ranging in age from 16 to 19. The females were Laotian (4), Japanese (2), and Vietnamese (1). The males were Caucasian and Laotian. The interview participants consisted of three males and two females between the ages of 15 and 18. The male participants were Laotian, Samoan, and Vietnamese. The female participants were Korean and Japanese.

The 87 participants who completed the questionnaire consisted of 49 males and 38 females. Four of the participants were in ninth grade, 13 in tenth grade, 62 in eleventh grade, and 6 in twelfth grade. Two of the students did not indicate their grade. The students identified their cultural backgrounds as Japanese (29), Hawaiian (13), Filipino (9), Caucasian (7), Chinese (5), Black (4), Samoan (3), Vietnamese (3), Korean (2), Thai (2), Micronesian (2), Hispanic (1), Laotian (1), Afghan/French (1), and mixed (1). Four participants were unsure of their cultural background and replied "don't know." The participants ranged in age from 14-19 with a mean age of 16.

To compare American youth with different ethnic/racial cultural roots, the questionnaires were separated into four groups based on geographic region and some traditional cultural similarities (Ji, Peng, & Nisbett, 2000). The four groups were East Asian (Japanese, Chinese, Korean) (n = 36), South-East Asian (Filipino, Thai, Vietnamese) (n = 14), Polynesian/Micronesian (n = 19), and Caucasian (n = 9). The four participants that indicated they were Black were dropped because there were not enough Black participants to constitute a fifth group. The four participants that were unsure of their background and replied "don't know" were also not included in the four groups.

## Measures

The focus group and the individual interviews were formatted to include the spectrum of peer group experiences[1] using a "prompt" style to elicit information about friends, types and times of activities with friends, and the importance of their friends and their friends' opinions. The questionnaire consisted of five measures: demographic information and scales assessing ethnocultural identity, attachment to peers, influence of peers, and activities with their peer group.[2]

*Demographic Measure.* The demographic measure consisted of questions on age, sex, grade in school, ethnicity/race of biological parents, and the culture that they identify with most.

*Ethnocultural Identity Behavioral Index.* The Ethnocultural Identity Behavioral Index (EIBI) is a validated scale extracted from the Multidimensional Ethnocultural Identification Scale (MEIS) (Oana & Marsella, 1979). The EIBI has been modified for use with multiple ethnocultural groups and measures the extent of involvement with one's cultural group (Yamada, Marsella, & Yamada, 1998). The scale consists of 19 behaviorally-based questions and one question assessing the "strength of identity" with the selected cultural group. These behavioral questions were rated on a Likert scale ranging from never (1) to always (6). The strength of identity question was also rated on a Likert scale ranging from very little (1) to very much (6).

*Assessing Peer Attachment.* To measure attachment to peers, the participants rated how often their friends encouraged them to do well in school, how often they confide in their peers and how often they would like to be the kind of person their friends are on a Likert scale ranging from never (1) to always (6).

*Assessing Peer Influence.* To assess peer influence, the participants rated how often they dress like peers, act like their peers, and consider how their friends will react before they act on a Likert scale ranging from never (1) to always (6).

*Assessing Peer Group Activities.* This measure assessed what the peer group does, when they participate in peer group activities, and with whom. The initiator of the activities, the roles of the peers involved, such as girlfriend or best friend, and demographic information about the peer group was also assessed.

### Procedure

The focus group participants were recruited from a YMCA-affiliated soccer program where high school students coach teams of younger players after school. All of the participants in the focus group were current soccer coaches and high school students. The focus group was conducted for 90 minutes in a classroom at Kaimuki High School. The head of the soccer program introduced the researcher, and asked the participants to help the researcher to understand what it is like to be a high school student.

The interview participants were recruited through a YMCA-affiliated program for high school students that were at-risk for academic failure. Each student was asked if they would be willing to participate. If they agreed, the participant was given a consent form to have signed by a parent. The participants were asked again for consent before the interview began. The interviews ranged from 30-55 minutes and were conducted in an office of the at-risk program. A counselor of the student introduced the students to the interviewer, and the interviewer explained the purpose of the study, and asked for the interviewee's help in understanding what it was like to be a teenager.

Both the interview and focus group participants were given McDonald's gift certificates in return for their participation. The 87 participants who completed the questionnaire were recruited from the chemistry classrooms at the same high school. Parental and individual consent were obtained for all participants prior to their participation in the study. The questionnaire was distributed by the interviewer and completed during class time. The teacher of the class introduced the researcher, and the researcher explained the purpose of the study and once again asked for the students' help in completing the survey in an honest and complete manner.

## RESULTS

### Focus Group and Interview Data

The focus group and interview data were read and re-read and phrases and sentences were coded. Codes were derived from the content of the phrase and captured the main point. The codes were then reviewed, comparing similarities, and combined into themes. The themes were reviewed and grouped into categories of themes based on similarities of ideas. Three categories emerged from the interview and focus group data: dynamics of peer group relationships, basis for peer group segmentation, and peer group problem-solving across several cultures.

The category of peer group dynamics was developed from themes stating that the participants experience and sometimes succumb to peer pressure (60%), yet think they do not act similar to peer group members and are independent (100%). These themes both expressed peer interaction within a group. The category of peer group segmentation became apparent from three themes stating that groups of friends are based on type of activity (80%), culture (80%), and neighborhood of people that "grew up together" (60%). These themes discussed the division of peer groups according to specific characteristics. The category of peer group problem-solving stemmed from themes that indicated that the participants tell their friends about their problems first (80%) because they trust them (80%), and that males tend to keep their problems to themselves or tell female confidants (60%). These themes addressed mechanisms through which peers work out their troubles.

### Questionnaire Data

Then MANOVA, ANOVAs, t-tests, and post-hoc tests were conducted, as appropriate, on the factor scores to identify cultural differences in peer group relationships, peer group demographics, and peer group activities.

*Peer Group Relationships, Attachment, and Influence.* Common factor analysis was conducted, with a promax oblique rotation, of the questionnaire measures of strength of cultural identity, peer attachment, and peer influence, to reduce the data and obtain factor scores for further analysis. The analysis resulted in the emergence of five factors with eigenvalues greater than one accounting for 57% of the variance. The first three factors, social interaction, language opportunities, and cultural activities, respectively, came from the measure of strength of cultural identity included in the EIBI. Factor 1, social interaction, described ways that individuals socialize within a specific cultural group. For example, a question that asked participants to rate on a Likert scale from never (1) to always (6) how often they "Interact frequently at informal gatherings with members of the group (e.g., parties, pot-lucks)" loaded highly on Factor 1. Factor 2, language opportunities, described opportunities for language exposure (i.e., "Speak the language of the group with my family and close friends"), and Factor 3, cultural activities, indicated participation in cultural group traditions and activities (i.e., "Participate in hobbies which are popular only within my group [e.g., origami, mah-jong]"). Factors four and five emerged from the measures of peer attachment (i.e., "How often do you spend time with your friends on the weekend?") and peer influence (i.e., "How often do you dress similar to your friends?"), respectively.

Individual factor scores were computed from the factor analysis, and a multivariate analysis of variance was conducted to see if there were factor score differences among the means of the four groups and the five factors. The multivariate analysis of variance indicated significant differences among groups, $F(3,75) = 2.20$ ($p < .01$), so one-way analyses of variance were conducted to determine the nature of these differences. Significant differences were found among groups on the factors labeled social interaction, $F(3,75) = 6.17$ ($p < .01$), language opportunities, $F(3,75) = 5.58$ ($p < .01$), and cultural activities, $F(3,75) = 4.63$ ($p < .01$). On a Likert scale of 1 (not attached/influenced) to 6 (very attached/influenced), the overall means for attachment ($M = 3.7$, $SD = .84$) and influence ($M = 3.7$, $SD = .96$) suggested that participants were moderately attached and influenced by their peer group. There were no significant differences among groups on factors of peer attachment and influence.

A post-hoc Games Howell analysis was used for social interaction means because the variance was heterogeneous. Tukey's HSD post-hoc analyses were used for language opportunities and cultural activities. Significant differences are presented in Table 1. Overall, the Polyne-

TABLE 1. Factor Score Means by Cultural Group

| Cultural Group | Factor 1 Mean | Factor 2 Mean | Factor 3 Mean | Factor 4 Mean | Factor 5 Mean |
|---|---|---|---|---|---|
| 1 East Asian | −0.024** | −0.048* | −0.122* | 0.125 | 0.012 |
| 2 South-East Asian | −0.772** | −0.708*** | −0.506** | −0.273 | −0.170 |
| 3 Polynesian | 0.337** | 0.517** | 0.499*** | −0.088 | −0.098 |
| 4 Caucasian | 0.426 | −0.173 | 0.195 | 0.101 | 0.145 |
| Significant Differences | 1 & 2, 2 & 3 | 1 & 2, 2 & 3 | 1 & 3, 2 & 3 | --- | --- |

Note: * Indicates that differences were found at the $p < .05$ level.
** Indicates that differences were found at the $p < .01$ level.
*** Indicates that differences were found at both the $p < .05$ and $p < .01$ level.

TABLE 2. Mean Rates of Participation in Significantly Different Peer Group Activities by Cultural Group

| Cultural Group | Organizational Activities | Reading | Mall | Unsupervised Partying | Concerts | Other |
|---|---|---|---|---|---|---|
| 1 East Asian | 14%*** | 14%* | 62%* | 17%** | 6%* | 8%** |
| 2 South-East Asian | 24%*** | 2%* | 69%* | 31% | 20% | 11%* |
| 3 Polynesian | 16%* | 4% | 39%*** | 49%** | 28%* | 7% |
| 4 Caucasian | 0%*** | 15% | 78%** | 22% | 7%* | 0%*** |
| Significant Differences | 3 & 4, 1 & 4, 2 & 4 | 1 & 2 | 1 & 3, 2 & 3, 3 & 4 | 1 & 3 | 1 & 3, 3 & 4 | 1 & 4, 2 & 4 |

Note: * Indicates that differences were found at the $p < .05$ level.
** Indicates that differences were found at the $p < .01$ level.
*** Indicates that differences were found at both the $p < .05$ and p $< .01$ level.

sian/Micronesian adolescents were highest and South-East Asian adolescents lowest on all three measures of cultural identification.

*Peer Group Activities.* Six a priori independent measure t-tests were also conducted to determine if there were differences in the types of activities of the groups. Activities during the day, night, weekend, and after school were summed and mean rates for each activity were calculated (i.e., mall, movies, organizational activities). As presented in Table 2, significant differences were found for organizational activities (clubs, teams, etc.), the mall, reading, unsupervised partying, and concerts.

Specifically, the East Asian cultural group was significantly different than Polynesians in time spent at the mall, $t(77) = 2.13, p < .05$, unsupervised partying, $t(77) = 3.28, p < .01$, and concerts $t(77) = 2.25, p < .05$, South-East Asians in reading, $t(77) = 1.96, p < .05$, and Caucasians in organizational activities, $t(77) = 2.76, p < .01$. South-East Asians were significantly different than Polynesians in time spent at the mall, $t(77) = 2.3, p < .05$, and Caucasians in organizational activities, $t(77) = 2.75, p < .05$. Polynesians were significantly different than Caucasians in organizational activities, $t(77) = 2.14, p < .05$, time spent at the mall, $t(77) = 2.8, p = .01$, and concerts, $t(77) = 2.03, p < .05$.

*Peer Group Demographics.* When asked about the extent of involvement with one's cultural group, participants indicated on a Likert scale of 1 (not involved) to 6 (very involved) that they were moderately involved with their cultural group ($M = 3.0, SD = .93$). When asked about the demographics of their peer group, participants indicated that they had between 0-45 friends ($M = 6.8, SD = 7.7$), with the number of male friends ($M = 3.6, SD = 6.2$) and female friends ($M = 3.2, SD = 5.5$) being very similar. Their friends ranged in age from 17-45 ($M = 16.6, SD = 4.4$) and were from a variety of cultural backgrounds: 68% of participants indicated that they had Hawaiian friends, 66% Chinese friends, 81% Japanese friends, 51% Caucasian friends, 47% Filipino friends, 23% Portuguese friends, 37% Korean friends, 18% Hispanic friends, 28% Samoan friends, 9% Tongan friends, 32% Black friends, 16% American Indian/Alaskan Native friends, and 13% Puerto Rican friends. Analyses of extent of involvement with one's cultural group, number of close friends, peer group ages and gender, and friend's cultural background did not reveal any significant differences.

To assess the potential of these results to understand group differences in delinquency, arrest rates for the four groups were calculated. First, the total number of arrests for each ethnicity was divided by the total number of arrests statewide for the ethnicities in each category to yield a percentage of statewide arrests for each ethnic group. Then the percentage of statewide arrests for each ethnic group was summed to provide a total arrest rate for each cultural group. Finally, the total arrest rate for each cultural group was divided by the percent of the population that the cultural group constituted to yield an arrest rate for each cultural group that was reflective of their representation in the corrections system in proportion to the representation in the general population. The arrest data were obtained from the 1999 FBI Uniform Crime Report (UCR, 1999). The Polynesian/Micronesian and South-East Asian groups were overrepresented with 328% and 134% arrest rates, respectively. The Caucasian and East Asian groups were underrepresented with 61% and 31% arrest rates, respectively.

The rates of participation in the types of peer group activities then were combined for the groups overrepresented in arrest rates (Polynesian/Micronesian and South-East Asian) and the underrepresented groups (Caucasian and East Asian) to see how activities corresponded to over- and-underrepresentation in arrest rates. An independent samples t-test was conducted and significant differences were found between the over- ($M = .08$, $SD = .28$) and underrepresented groups for the activities of reading, ($M = .42$, $SD = .99$), $t(77) = 2.07$, $p < .05$, unsupervised partying, (over $M = 1.24$, $SD = 1.13$), (under $M = .53$, $SD = .92$), $t(77) = -2.96$, $p < .01$, and concert attendance, (over $M = .74$, $SD = 1.11$), (under $M = .20$, $SD = .59$), $t(77) = -2.56$, $p = .01$.

## DISCUSSION

The goal of this study was to gain insight into the relationship between culture, peer group relationships, and delinquency. Support was found for group differences in cultural identification, participation in the youth culture, and the importance of activities in understanding delinquency. Group differences in cultural identification were strongest between the Polynesian/Micronesian and South-East Asian groups. Yet these groups were both overrepresented on group arrest rates, making it unlikely that cultural identification, per se, could explain differences in delinquency.

Participation in the youth culture was supported by the lack of group differences in peer attachment, peer influence, and peer demographics (number of close friends, extent of involvement with one's cultural group, friend's cultural background, peer group ages, gender). The lack of these differences among the four groups suggests the similarity of peer relations, regardless of cultural differences. This similarity was also supported by the focus group/interview data where the students reported that they experience and sometimes succumb to peer pressure, share the value of independence, and tell their friends about their problems first because they trust them. Their greater reliance on friends rather than family is a characteristic of the youth culture.

The importance of independence in youth culture is consistent with the ideals prominent in Western culture. The pervasive nature of this theme across the four cultures represented in this study indicates the Westernization of these cultures in Hawaii, even among the Polynesian/Micronesian adolescents who were highest on the measures of cultural identification.

However, participation in a common youth culture cannot, of course, explain the group differences in arrest rates. The data suggest, however, that some activities may help to do so. The focus group/interview data showed that activities were the basis for peer group formation as much as cultural background and common neighborhoods, and rates of participation in three of these activities, unsupervised partying, concerts, and reading, matched the pattern of arrest rates among the four groups and showed significant differences when the four groups were combined in those over- and-underrepresented in arrest rates.

Joined with independence is a unique set of peer group norms. Consequently, a new set of values, addressing age-related concerns and perceptions of adulthood, are established and a group identity is formed (Corsaro, 1985). These norms can be linked to the reliance on peer groups for problem-solving. The participants described peers as their only confidants when they encountered a problem. Utilizing the peers as a vital reference point is a clear indicator of the existence and pervasiveness of a youth culture where "school becomes the center where the adolescent comes to focus on his peer group as a vital reference point" (Gottlieb & Ten Houten, 1966).

Furthermore, traditional culture does not have an effect on peer group relationships and therefore cannot be used to protect adolescents from the mediating power of the peer group. The set of values perpetuated by the youth culture more accurately addresses age-related concerns and the group identity formed by this youth culture may be more pervasive during adolescence than traditional culture.

The data indicated that type of activity may play a role in delinquency. Although peer group segmentation may be based on cultural group differences and neighborhoods, certain activities were linked with delinquent behavior. The groups overrepresented in arrest rates, Polynesian/Micronesian and South-East Asian adolescents spent less time reading and more time in unsupervised parties and concerts than the underrepresented groups, East Asian and Caucasian adolescents. These findings are consistent with activity setting theory and suggest the value of intervention strategies that focus on the activities of adolescents (O'Donnell, Tharp, & Wilson, 1993).

Therefore, although membership in the cultural group per se may not be related directly to arrests, activities encouraged by cultural groups may deter or facilitate delinquent activity. Activities such as reading may serve to deter, while unsupervised partying and concert attendance may facilitate delinquent activity. Reading, of course, is typically a solo activity, while partying and concert attendance are peer group activities. Lack of supervision is one of the most important variables associated with delinquency (e.g., Wilson, 1980).

The significance of youth culture also suggests the value of focusing on the role of peer groups in delinquency (O'Donnell, Manos, & Chesney-Lind, 1987). Specifically, knowledge of youth culture and the development of prevention strategies based on peer groups could result in more effective prevention of juvenile delinquency. Currently, few prevention and intervention programs are peer-based (Tolan & Guerra, 1994).

An important limitation of this study is that individual arrest data for the participants was not available. Therefore, the arrest data compiled from statewide arrest rates may not be representative of the cultural groups. Follow-up research collecting individual arrest data, including a representative percentage of incarcerated juveniles, should be conducted.

## NOTES

1. A copy of the prompts utilized in the interviews and focus groups can be obtained by contacting the author at Department of Psychology, University of Hawaii at Manoa, Honolulu, HI 96822.

2. A copy of the questionnaire can be obtained by contacting the author at Department of Psychology, University of Hawaii at Manoa, Honolulu, HI 96822.

## REFERENCES

Adler, F. & Laufer, W. S. (Eds.). (1995). *The legacy of anomie theory.* New Brunswick, NJ: Transaction.

Agnew, R. (1993). Why do they do it? An examination of the intervening mechanisms between social control variables and delinquency. *Journal of Research in Crime and Delinquency, 30,* 245-266.

Arnold, M. E. & Hughes, J. N. (1999). First do no harm: Adverse effects of grouping deviant youth for skills training. *Journal of School Psychology, 37,* 99-115.

Banerjee, M. (1997). Peeling the onion: A multi-layered view of children's emotional development. In S. Hala (Ed.), *The development of social cognition. Studies in developmental psychology* (pp. 241-272). Hove, England: Psychology Press, Erlbaum, Taylor & Francis.

Beccaria, C. (1974). *On crimes and punishments.* New York, NY: Bobbs-Merrill.

Booth, A. & Osgood, D. W. (1993). The influence of testosterone on deviance in adulthood: Assessing and explaining the relationship. *Criminology, 31*, 93-117.

Bursik, R. J. (1988). Social disorganization and theories of crime and delinquency: Problems and prospects. *Criminology, 26*, 519-551.

Carey, G. (1992). Twin imitation for antisocial behavior: Implications for genetic and family environment research. *Journal of Abnormal Psychology, 101*, 18-25.

Cloninger, C. R. & Gottesman, I. I. (1987). Genetic and environmental factors in anti-social behavior disorders. In S. Mednick, T. Moffitt & S. Stack (Eds.), *The causes of crime: New biological approaches* (pp. 92-109). New York, NY: Cambridge University Press.

Coie, J. D., Terry, R., Zakriski, A., & Lochman, J. (1995). In J. McCord (Ed.), *Coercion and punishment in long-term perspectives* (pp. 229-244). New York, NY: Cambridge University Press.

Corsaro, W. A. (1985). *Friendship and peer culture in the early years.* Norwood, NJ: Ablox.

Dishion, T. J., McCord, J., & Poulin, F. (1999). When interventions harm: Peer groups and problem behavior. *American Psychologist, 54*, 755-764.

Emler, N., Reicher, S., & Ross, A. (1987). The social context of delinquent conduct. *Journal of Child Psychology and Psychiatry, 28*, 99-109.

Friedman, H. L. (1993). Adolescent social development: A global perspective: Implications for health promotion across cultures. *Journal of Adolescent Health, 14*, 588-594.

Gardner, L. & Shoemaker, D. J. (1994). Social bonding and delinquency: A comparative analysis. *Sociological Quarterly, 30*, 481-500.

Gottlieb, D. J. & Ten Houten, W. (1966). *The emergence of youth societies: A cross-cultural approach.* New York, NY: The Free Press.

Horwitz, A. & Wasserman, M. (1980). Some misleading conceptions in sentencing research: An example of a reformulation in the juvenile court. *Criminology, 18*, 411-424.

Ji, L., Peng, K., & Nisbett, R. (2000). Culture, control, and perception of relationships in the environment. *Journal of Personality and Social Psychology, 78*, 943-955.

Lyerly, R. R. & Skipper, J. K. (1981). Differential rates of rural urban delinquency: A social control approach. *Criminology, 29*, 397-417.

McCarthy, B. R. & Smith, B. L. (1986). The conceptualization of discrimination in the juvenile justice process: The impact of administrative factors and screening decisions on juvenile court dispositions. *Criminology, 24*, 41-64.

Mednick, S.A., Gabrielli, W., & Hutchings, B. (1987). Genetic factors in the etiology of criminal behavior. In S. Mednick, T. Moffitt & S. Stack (Eds.), *The causes of crime: New biological approaches* (pp. 74-91). New York, NY: Cambridge University Press.

Oana, L. & Marsella, A.J. (1979). The multidimensional measurement of ethnocultural identity in Japanese-Americans. Unpublished manuscript, University of Hawaii at Manoa.

O'Donnell, C. R., Manos, M. J., & Chesney-Lind, M. (1987). Diversion and neighborhood delinquency programs in open settings: A social network interpretation. In E. K. Morris & C. J. Braukman (Eds.), *Behavioral approaches to crime and delinquency: Application, research and theory* (pp. 251-269). New York: Plenum Press.

O'Donnell, C. R., Tharp, R. G., & Wilson, K. (1993). Activity settings as the unit of analysis: A theoretical basis for community intervention and development. *American Journal of Community Psychology, 21*, 501-520.

Ray, M. C. & Downs, W. R. (1986). An empirical test of labeling theory using longitudinal data. *Journal of Research in Crime and Delinquency, 23*, 169-194.

Sampson, R. J. (1994). Urban poverty and the family context of delinquency: A new look at structure and process in a classic study. *Child Development, 65*, 523-540.

Schlegel, A. & Barry, H. (1991). *Adolescence: An anthropological inquiry*. New York, NY: The Free Press.

Snyder, H. (2001). *1999 Juvenile Arrests*. Washington DC: Office of Juvenile Justice and Delinquency Prevention, U.S. Department of Justice.

Tanioka, I. & Glaser, D. (1991). School uniforms, routine activities, and the social control of delinquency in Japan. *Youth and Society, 23*, 50-75.

Thomas, C. W. & Bishop, D. M. (1984). The effect of formal and informal sanctions on delinquency: A longitudinal comparison of labeling and deterrence theories. *The Journal of Law and Criminology, 75*, 1222-1245.

Tolan, P. H. & Guerra, N. G. (1994). Prevention of delinquency: Current status and issues. *Applied & Preventive Psychology, 3*, 251-273.

Uniform Crime Report, Federal Bureau of Investigation. (1999). *Crime in Hawaii, 1999*, Retrieved September 1, 2001, from http://www.cpja.ag.state.hi.us/ccp/

Vega, W., Khoury, E., Zimmerman, R., Gil, A., & Warheit, G. (1995). Cultural conflicts and problem behaviors of Latino adolescents in home and school environments. *Journal of Community Psychology, 23*, 167-179.

Wall, J., Power, T., & Arbona, C. (1993). Susceptibility to antisocial peer pressure and its relation to acculturation in Mexican-American adolescents. *Journal of Adolescent Research, 8*, 403-418.

Wells, L. E. (1991). Families and delinquency: A meta-analysis of the impact of broken homes. *Social Problems, 38*, 71-93.

White, H. R., Pandina, R. J., & LaGrange, R. L. (1987). Longitudinal predictors of serious substance use and delinquency. *Criminology, 25*, 715-740.

Wilson, H. (1980). Parental supervision: A neglected aspect of delinquency. *British Journal of Criminology, 20*, 203-235.

Wong, S. K. (1999). Acculturation, peer relations, and delinquent behavior of Chinese-Canadian youth. *Adolescence, 34*, 108-119.

Yamada, A., Marsella, A.J., & Yamada, S.Y. (1998). The development of the ethnocultural identity behavioral index: Psychometric properties and validation with Asian Americans and Pacific Islanders. *Asian American and Pacific Islander Journal of Health, 6*(1), 36-45.

# Juvenile Delinquency in Japan

Yuko Yamamiya

*University of South Florida*

**SUMMARY.** Juvenile delinquency in Japan is examined with respect to Japanese culture. The cultural changes in Japan since World War II, and especially since 1970, have affected family, school, neighborhood, and peer relationships. Changes in juvenile delinquency are presented and discussed within the context of these historical and cultural changes in Japanese society. *[Article copies available for a fee from The Haworth Document Delivery Service: 1-800-HAWORTH. E-mail address: <docdelivery@ haworthpress.com> Website: <http://www.HaworthPress.com> © 2003 by The Haworth Press, Inc. All rights reserved.]*

**KEYWORDS.** Delinquency, Japan, culture, peers, community

Juvenile delinquency is one of the most pervasive problems in modern and urbanized Japanese society. Increasing numbers of youth crimes are

Yoko Yamamiya came to the United States from Japan in 1994, and completed her BA degree at the University of Hawaii and MS degree at the Old Dominion University, Norfolk, VA. Currently, she is in the Clinical Psychology PhD program at the University of South Florida. Her current research interests are body-image disturbances among young populations across different cultures and social factors that influence body-image development

Address correspondence to: Yuko Yamamiya, University of South Florida, Department of Psychology, 4202 E. Fowler Avenue, PCD4118G, Tampa, FL 33620.

[Haworth co-indexing entry note]: "Juvenile Delinquency in Japan." Yamamiya, Yuko. Co-published simultaneously in *Journal of Prevention & Intervention in the Community* (The Haworth Press, Inc.) Vol. 25, No. 2, 2003, pp. 27-46; and: *Culture, Peers, and Delinquency* (ed: Clifford R. O'Donnell) The Haworth Press, Inc., 2003, pp. 27-46. Single or multiple copies of this article are available for a fee from The Haworth Document Delivery Service [1-800-HAWORTH, 9:00 a.m. - 5:00 p.m. (EST). E-mail address: docdelivery@haworthpress.com].

27

reported and Japanese youth seem to be increasingly violent. Violence has been referred to as a fad among teenagers who respect violent peers (The Word of Children, 1997).

Some Japanese youth develop a complex symptom called tokokyohi (school refusal) or hikikomori (self-confinement), which is a widespread concern in Japan (Vogel, 1996). It is a total withdrawal from current society. Typically, a child stops attending school, withdraws himself (herself) to his room, avoids any contact with the outside world, sleeps during the daytime, and watches television or videos at night. It often involves parent abuse as well. The child destroys things around the house and batters his parents, particularly his mother. These children often commit other violent crimes as well.

A survey of 7,000 high school students showed that 13% of high school students abuse alcohol, over 50% of junior high school students and 85% of high school students read pornographic books, and a notable number of girls who attend some of the most privileged high schools have posed in pornographic videos, sold their underwear to a pornographic producer, or prostituted for allowance money. Moreover, contemporary Japanese youth subculture is saturated with violence, which is often associated with erotic overtones (Bayley, 1991). Cartoon magazines for boys, for instance, depict images of their "mothers composed of feces, boys breaking wind in the faces of their fathers, [and] hydra-penised monsters committing multiple rape of schoolgirls" (Naff, 1994, p. 221). Videos containing images of mutilated corpses from the war in former Yugoslavia, death scenes from disastrous car wrecks, and pictures of decomposing bodies with split skulls are stocked in local video shops.

The dramatic transformation of Japanese society into affluent modern life, with feelings of emptiness and apathy among youths, is often blamed for causing a bizarre youth subculture (Naff, 1994). The suicide rate among children has increased (Hara & Minagawa, 1996) and many Japanese young people report not liking themselves (Kawasaki & Haga, 1995).

To understand juvenile delinquency in Japan, it is necessary to look at the nation's physical and historical characteristics as well as social and cultural values over time, because juvenile delinquency is a social phenomenon that gradually emerges from a changing society. Japan is 30 times as densely populated as the United States, and is one of the most crowded countries in the world (Westermann & Burfeind, 1991). The majority of its people are a blend of Eastern Asian peoples who had immigrated to Japan centuries ago (Reischauer, 1988), yet most Japanese perceive themselves as ethnically pure and homogeneous (Westermann & Burfeind, 1991). The written history of Japan can be traced back more than 1,400 years. Throughout its history, a hierarchy and complex ranking system became the main political structure and gave direction for human relationships. The Japanese recognize the power of authority and value subservience and obligation, in contrast to the American values of individual rights, equality, and freedom (Clifford, 1976). Democracy was not introduced until the 1890s.

In the 1970s, Japan experienced modernization associated with population growth, urbanization, industrialization, democratization, and high mass consumption (Kawasaki, 1994). Modernization resulted in an affluent society with a new, advanced consumption culture, dominated by youth, and associated with the consumption of expensive foods and designer clothes (Kawasaki & Haga, 1995). The solid economic success and societal affluence allowed the nation, especially the younger population, to be more individualistic than ever (Kawasaki & Haga, 1995; Yamaguchi, 1994). However, among the young there was widespread apathy (Shindo et al., 1993), a poisonous cynicism accompanied by egocentricity (Naff, 1994), and social virtues such as effort and serious-mindedness have faded (Naka, 1977). Although the Japanese still felt a strong national identity, they were far less patriotic (Naff, 1994).

Most Japanese were proud of the national economic success in this era (Naff, 1994), but many people also felt doubt, agony, or anger at the paths the nation had taken in order to achieve it. For instance, speculators hired gangsters to expel citizens from their lands and politicians attained wealth through bribery (Befu, 1971). Although consumerism pervaded society and most Japanese seemed rich, there was a wide gap between haves and have-nots (Naff, 1994). Everyone was employed and thousands of Japanese literally worked themselves to death as their vacation time decreased and working hours increased; yet few people could ever afford to own a house. Consequently, certain social norms or values came to be perceived as unjust (Bertrand, 1972).

At the same time, large numbers of young people moved into cities. The percentage of the young population who lived in the six major cities increased from 19% in 1960 to 40% in the early 1970s (Naka, 1977). Those who had moved from tradition-bound communities to the urban areas, however, soon found themselves in the middle of agitation from the cities' sudden and rapid changes. Self-direction became more valued and the stresses and strains arising from the rapid change in social structure became acute.

As the nation proceeded into the 1990s, numerous disgraceful schemes between big business and politicians were revealed to the public. For instance, big companies were secretly refunded their losses from the great Tokyo stock crash of 1990, while many citizens suffered from losing their life savings (Naff, 1994). Not surprisingly, the public felt abused by the plots and by the sudden blow-up of a "bubble economy," both of which appeared to be part of a conspiracy of the "big people."

Economically, the distribution of wealth in Japan is relatively equal compared to other nations, including the United States (Bayley, 1991). Impoverishment and homelessness do exist, but there are few slums, or areas of "chronic poverty, unemployment, family pathology, and high crime" (Bayley, 1991, p. 170) and no ghettos, or chronically impoverished areas with "members of groups that are subjected to discrimination by the general population" (p. 170). Moreover, Japan does not have any large, well-defined, and competitive religious, ethnic, or cultural diversity. In sum, Japan does not have the characteristics that often create "economic inequality to produce successive generations of the misery, hopelessness, rage, and family disintegration that are so strongly associated with crime" (Bayley, 1991, p. 171). Thus, despite the urbanization, overpopulation, and industrialization that are often associated with delinquency, Japan still has the lowest crime and delinquency rate among industrialized countries (Savells, 1991). Some sociologists argue that it is a reflection of Japan's residual, familial, political, philosophical, and traditional norms and values. However, these values seem to be changing among the young and these changes are the source of much concern about delinquency.

## TRADITIONAL JAPANESE VALUES

Japan's traditional cultural values are often said to be one of social control of delinquency, as they regulate the way social relationships are expressed. Japanese culture typifies that of a very small, geographically isolated nation (Kawasaki, 1994), and Japan's physical isolation and self-imposed seclusion from the 17th to the 19th century A.D. have made it possible to establish one of the most unified and homogeneous societies in the world (Ames, 1981). Homogeneity plays an especially important role in social control (Forbis, 1975). In Japanese society, the social structure of every group is homogeneous, based on shared principles (Hata & Smith, 1983).

The small group composes Japanese society with simultaneous links with the larger society, inferring that those who do not, or cannot, belong to any small group are unable to live in Japanese society. The sense of belonging to a group also determines one's sense of individuality, self-identity, and self-concept (Burks, 1981; Masatsugu, 1982; Wagatsuma & Rosett, 1986; Westermann & Burfeind, 1991). How a person behaves in social contexts is strongly determined by his or her self-concept as a member of a group (Triandis, Kagitcibasi, Choi, & Yoon, 1989). People's feelings of self-worth also depends on the regard and acknowledgement they receive from the group to which they belong (Masatsugu, 1982). As a result, individualism is expressed through shared action and membership, whereas self-identity is developed through group interaction. For this reason, ostracism, or nakama hazure, has been one of the severest punishments in Japan (Nakane, 1978).

The notion of nakama, or peers, is very important to the Japanese. Equality is presumed and preferred among nakama, even in physical and mental ability (Yamaguchi, 1990). The fundamental relation within nakama is, "We are the same" (Inoue, 1977). If any unequal relation is introduced, the nakama will break up immediately. Of course, total equality among nakama does not always exist in reality and each member in the group has his or her territory and status, which is often determined by occupational position based on education (Masatsugu, 1982).

This importance of nakama is closely related to collectivism (Yamaguchi, 1994), which has been induced and facilitated by the historical agricultural system of the nation–rice cultivation. The most important aspect in rice cultivation is cooperation, not competition. In order for a village to survive, individual desires or demands must be put aside and only when villagers work cooperatively with others can their best interests be achieved. Though individualism has become strong in Japan since the early 1980s (Kawasaki & Haga, 1995), the Japanese are still far more collectivistic than Americans.

Collectivism emphasizes the priority of group goals, leading collectivists to withhold their personal opinions, favors, and even emotions when these differ from those of a group (Yamaguchi, 1994). Instead, collectivists learn to be sensitive and attentive to what other group members expect or they will lose positive reputations as members of the group. Araki (1973) states that the Japanese are taught to fulfill the group's demands and to conform to the group opinions from birth. For older generations, "harmony" is still an important human value; for younger generations, "harmony" is maintained in order to prevent invasion of their privacy.

When the sense of belonging to a group, along with loyalty and attachment, becomes too strong, it often results in indifference or hostility toward the out-group (Inoue, 1977), especially when the membership is inclusive and the size of the group is small. Sometimes the difference between members and nonmembers appear so huge that nonmembers are considered as less than human, while individual differences within a group are almost ignored in the name of "harmony" (Inoue, 1977). The hostility towards the out-group then strengthens the bond among members in the in-group.

The Japanese are especially sensitive to the constant change between themselves and others based on the status of the others on a continuum with two end-points: soto, outside, and uchi, inside (Greenfield & Cocking, 1994; Kondo, 1990). Uchi is the realm people belong to and soto is the rest, and the Japanese create their sphere of life in accordance with the division between uchi and soto (Inoue, 1977). These terms entreat "a complex series of graduations along a scale of detachment and engagement, distance and intimacy, formality and informality" (Kondo, 1990, p. 31). People learn to be submissive and respectful in the soto situation, but may act differently in the uchi situation. For instance, modes of speech must be different based on whom one speaks to in order to avoid offending (Bayley, 1991). To recognize the extent to which uchi behavior is proper in a certain situation is one of the important social skills.

The different roles that a person has to play depending on situations may cause a conflict (Kato, 1977). People may have some inner problems or struggles, but they maintain their positive appearance in public. To maintain seken-tei, or the appearance and the sense of righteousness in the public eye, is extremely important in Japan. Seken is very close to a reference group, based on which the Japanese decide their behaviors and attitude (Inoue, 1977).

The "other-oriented" tendency makes the Japanese very sensitive to what is going on within seken, thus eager to control how they are regarded (Inoue, 1977). How they externally appear to seken is thought to reflect a person's inner state of mind (Greenfield & Cocking, 1994). For example, a messy dressing style is considered as a manifestation of looseness of mind. In turn, appearance can inwardly "seep in" to influence the mind. Thus, imposition of precise rules of external manners corresponds to "spiritual" education in Japan. In Japanese schools, for instance, students' external conduct including "the length of hair, . . . minimum physical distance between boy and girl in conversation, [and] prohibition of cosmetics and perms" (Greenfield & Cocking, 1994, p. 264) are strictly controlled. All students must wear the same uniform with the same length of skirt or width of pants and carry identical bags (Bayley, 1991; Greenfield & Cocking, 1994). Since the Japanese believe they are what they look like, they have to conform to the appearance of what they want to be (Bayley, 1991) in order to be accepted by seken.

The Japanese mothers are the central socialization agents, and the bond between the mother and the child is considered the basis of all human relationships (Tanaka, 1986; Wagatsuma & De Vos, 1984). Therefore, the child's future is thought to be closely related to maternal practices (e.g., Tronick, Morelli, & Ivey, 1992).

Even the norms and rules strictly followed in the yakuza underworld are strongly connected to the highly valued traditions in Japan. The most salient aspect of yakuza is called jingi (Ames, 1981). Jingi is the code of morality, which requires a follower to display absolute loyalty and obedience to the gang leader. At the same time, the gang leader is expected to make sure proper care and protection are provided to his followers. Their ideology is clearly derived from the traditional national ideology, which has been lost in the rest of Japanese society (Ames, 1981). Juvenile gangs often use this yakuza ideology to strengthen the ties among group members.

Members of the yakuza are usually drawn from the lowest social strata that frequently suffer discrimination, both socially and economically (Ames, 1981; Clifford, 1976; Kelly, 1986). As youths, they have been delinquents who are alienated and rejected by the broader society. They are often the failures and dropouts who have little chance to be a respected member in the larger society (Westermann & Burfeind, 1991). Partially due to their poor familial background, they have experienced rejection from larger society since childhood, depriving them of the opportunity to find secure jobs when they get older. As a result, more than 50% of them are unemployed and 40% are economically insecure when they join the yakuza. In addition, many of them run away from home (43%) or become financially independent from their family at a very early age (Ames, 1981). Therefore, the yakuza group is often a surrogate for young people who cannot be members of the larger society (Ames, 1981; Westermann & Burfeind, 1991).

Far fewer police are employed in Japan compared to the United States (Vago, 1988) and Japan spends considerably less on police, courts, and corrections (Bayley, 1991). Japanese police serve in a wide range of activities such as the resolution of domestic disputes, prevention of crime, and enforcement of laws (Bayley, 1976a, 1976b). The policing system in Japan possesses all of the characteristics of community policing. The close relationship that Japanese police have with local community is one of the reasons for their effectiveness.

Each police station has a juvenile unit responsible for youth problems (Ames, 1981). There are 2,000 or more police-school liaison councils, which encompass 90% of all elementary and middle schools in Japan (Bayley, 1991). Also, nearly 5,000 counselors are appointed specifically to juvenile guidance by the Prefectual Public Safety Commission, who work with volunteers to provide advice as well as support to juveniles in trouble or categorized as "pre-delinquent." They are mostly teachers, parents, and juvenile probation officers (Ames, 1981; Bayley, 1991). Their primary objective is to prevent delinquency by catching youths before they turn into career juvenile offenders (Ames, 1981). The police juvenile unit also offers counseling to both juveniles and their parents (Ames, 1981; Bayley, 1991).

The juvenile unit uses a method known as "street guidance." Juvenile officers patrol places where adolescents are likely to gather–shopping malls, parks, train stations, pachinko parlors, game centers, and fast food restaurants (Ames, 1981; Bayley, 1991). During the day, they look for truants; at night, they look for young runaways and juveniles who engage in improper activities, such as smoking, "hanging out" in school uniform, playing in game centers after dark, and wearing too long or too short skirts and having permed or colored hair. Smoking in public is thought to be the most serious transgression of all; in Japan, smoking is considered the first sign to indicate a child's delinquent tendency (the law in Japan prohibits those under the age of 20 from smoking) (Bayley, 1991). When the juvenile unit finds a youth engaging in such undesirable activities, they quietly approach the youth, warning him or her to stop the behavior immediately (Ames, 1981; Bayley, 1991). In street guidance, elementary and middle schools become the central concern (Bayley, 1991). Warning youths that their schools will be notified is an effective threat to them, because it would put them under strict supervision.

Legal culture, or people's beliefs, ideas, and expectations for the legal system, is less punitive in sentencing in Japan (Friedman, 1984). The use of informal social control is preferred to punishment whenever possible (Suzuki, 1979). Also, there is a skeptical attitude toward the effectiveness of imprisonment as a means of rehabilitation. Thus, even when punishment is necessary, community-based treatment is preferred.

Japanese judges are also lenient in sentencing a criminal offender as well (Reischauer, 1988; Tanizawa, 1979). Compared to the United States, much more lenient sentences are given for similar crimes (Bayley, 1991). Judges do not think that mere severity in sentencing meets the primary objective of punishment. Rather, leniency functions as a vehicle for rehabilitation because the judge's benevolence makes the offender feel indebted (Tanizawa, 1979). Also, the sentence itself is not the effective punishment in Japanese culture because being convicted for a crime, which brings shame to family and friends, is punishment in and of itself, for social control is based on shame in Japan (Clifford, 1976).

In order to resocialize offenders, work is considered the central activity and fundamental means (Clifford, 1976). Work not only provides knowledge and skill, but also increases self-reliance and cooperation among the offenders (Corrections Bureau, 1982). In addition, work can teach offenders cultural values such as harmony and group-relatedness.

Psychological counseling is never part of the rehabilitative correctional system in Japan (Westermann & Burfeind, 1991). However, Naikan therapy has been used, especially with juvenile offenders since the 1960s (Matsumoto et al., 1978). Naikan therapy came from Zen meditation and is based on introspection. Offenders contemplate their past mischief, other people's expectations, and their own obligations to other people in self-imposed isolation. This therapy emphasizes moral responsibility and cultural values in Japanese society (Clifford, 1976).

## CHANGES IN DELINQUENCY SINCE 1970

As social systems change, the types of delinquent subcultures change as well (Bell, 1971). Japan experienced its most rapid cultural and societal changes from 1970 to 2000. Juvenile crimes started to increase after 1973 and by 1975 accounted for 32% of all arrests (Ames, 1981).

In 1975, 74% of crimes committed by juveniles involved theft, of which about half were simple cases such as shoplifting, motorcycle/bicycle theft, and auto theft (Ames, 1981; Naka, 1977). Serious crimes, such as robbery, rape, and burglary, frequently involved automobile gangs called bosozoku ("reckless driving tribes") (Ames, 1981). Unlike the student radicals in the 1970s, bosozoku youths formed groups based on physical and sensation needs such as excitement and speed rather than ideology (Tamura, 1989). The "motorization" of the nation appeared to be the key to the expansion and diversification of crimes in Japan (Naka, 1977). In addition, Bayley (1991) found that criminal offenses against teachers and school property started to increase in the late 1970s. These offenses were often based on ideology with the core members of the group often "fanatical in their antipathy for the ruling political and economic establishment in Japan–especially the police force" (Ames, 1981, p. 86). The use of drugs including glue and paint thinner also became a problem among youths in the 1970s (Ames, 1981; Bayley, 1991).

The number of the juvenile arrests for assault came to a peak in 1981, as did extortion in 1986 (Research and Training Institute Ministry of Justice, 1997). Children's violence was mainly aimed at school or family (Naff, 1994). Some attributed this increase in delinquency to lax parental childrearing (Shindo et al., 1993).

The average age of delinquents has continued to decline to below 15 years old (Shindo et al., 1993), while the number of serious, violent crimes by juveniles has been increasing at an alarming rate (Regoli & Hewitt, 1997). Even deviant behavior in "ordinary" children has become more acceptable. Japanese children consider those who are usually calm, but become uncontrollably violent only occasionally as "hip" (The Word of Children, 1997). In fact, many heroes in Japanese cartoons or comics display such convulsive rage and violence.

This violence is typically a male phenomenon (Regoli & Hewitt, 1997) because boys' violence is more tolerated than girls' in Japan (Boys with Knives, 1997). Also, while girls can express their feelings with words, boys cannot do the same, for talking too much is thought to be "sissy" in Japan. Most boys report a desire to use violence against those who yell at or make fun of them, ignore them, do not understand them, or prevent them from doing something, and many admit the desire to use violence without any reason or purpose (Takahashi & Kobayashi, 1989).

Murder cases committed by students with compulsive anger have become widespread in Japan during the last few years (Research and Training Institute Ministry of Justice, 1997). Sixty-five percent of juveniles who murdered their acquaintances were between 14 and 15 years old (Watanabe, Tamura, & Kurusu, 1995). Of those who murdered their relatives, more than 50% stabbed their victims, while those who murdered either an acquaintance or a stranger were more likely to beat the person to death (Watanabe et al., 1995).

A large number of juveniles have been arrested for using drugs and inhalants in the 1990s as well (Shindo et al., 1993). The use of glue has been common, the use of amphetamines, tranquilizers, and cocaine is on the rise (Naff, 1994), and the recidivism of glue sniffing is higher than that of other illegal activities (Suzuki, Inokuchi, Watanabe, Kobayashi, Okeda, & Takahashi, 1995). Those who sniff glue by themselves are often apathetic and have problems in human relationships, while those who sniff glue with peers are often members of a gang or group with multiple criminal records (Suzuki et al., 1995).

Factors that may help us to understand these trends in delinquency since the 1970s are discussed below. These include family, school, and peer factors.

*Family Factors*

The birth rate of Japan dramatically dropped after World War II. During the 1970s, it fell below the optimal reproduction level of 2.08 (Koseisho, 1998). The birthrate kept on dropping and eventually declined to 1.34 in 2001 (Orenstein, 2001). The number of children who are under 15 years old declines by over 500,000 each year and is now only 14.64% of the population, the lowest in the world (CIA, 2001). As a result, today's children have fewer, if any, siblings (Chen, 1996; Hara & Minagawa, 1996). Thus, they spend more time by themselves, watching television, playing Nintendo, or attending a cram school. This generation of children is growing up without developing the ability to properly interact with peers (Chen, 1996). With fewer children, parents are deprived of an opportunity to develop different perspectives on children and widen their knowledge of individual differences. The parents' attention and expectations are heavily concentrated on their only child.

Consequently, the number of family members in one household decreased as well. In 1991, the average family size became as low as three, and nuclear families and single-person households made up 80.8% of the total households (Kumagai, 1995). If both parents have a job, the child is left unsupervised at home (Ames, 1981). While the mothers of nondelinquents are mostly housewives, those of delinquents work outside the home (Koyama, 1973). In addition, since today's nuclear family is strongly tied to the demands of outside institutions such as company and school (White, 1996) and the bond within the nuclear family itself is weak (Ames, 1981), the function of a family is limited to a base to support school and work (White, 1996). Indeed, the traditional objectives of a family–companionship, affection, and happiness–are replaced with the fulfillment of social and economic demands (Naff, 1994).

As the delinquency level of a child goes up, the social class of the family seems to go down; a youth who commits a serious crime tends to come from a family of low social-economic status or is dysfunctional. For instance, juveniles who murdered their relatives are likely to have abusive or alcoholic parents (Watanabe et al., 1995). Also, many juveniles who killed their acquaintances are from one-parent families without the biological father (Watanabe et al., 1995). When juveniles start their deviancy early in age, their family background tends to be lower, too; most of their parents have a blue-collar job. Furthermore, about half of juveniles arrested during middle school years have a breadwinner whose last educational achievement is below middle school (Harada, 1992).

In Japan, delinquency, especially among boys, takes place in families where there is little internal cohesion, poor supervision, inconsistent discipline, and lack of affection (Wagatsuma & De Vos, 1984). The overall relationship between parents and the child is more remote when the child is delinquent. The parents of delinquents celebrate the child's birthday less, participate in the child's school events less, and talk less in daily life compared to those of nondelinquents (Koyama, 1973; Uchiyama & Inokuchi, 1995).

Child abuse has become another problem in the Japanese family. The number of alcoholic parents is growing in Japan. The Ministry of Health and Welfare found that overall 11.9% of men and 1.7% of women were "problem drinkers"; this means there are 8.4 million alcohol abusers (Naff, 1994). The children raised by alcohol abusers often join or form groups with other children, who are in similar situations, and engage in delinquency together (Sato, 1997a). When delinquents and nondelinquents are compared, fewer delinquents want to spend time with their parents and more want to spend time with older youths in the community (Hoshino et al., 1995).

## School Factors

The mother's total devotion to her child often leads her to be a frantically education-minded mother, known as kyoiku-mama (Kumagai, 1995). The kyoiku-mama, representing 60 to 70% of Japanese mothers, is profoundly preoccupied with the education of her child (particularly her son), especially his performance on school entrance exams (Azuma, 1994). Since a housewife's status in Japan is largely determined by her success in leading her son to "win" the race, the mother steers her son through massive competition to enter a "good" university that produces a few winners and millions of losers (Kumagai, 1995). Japanese children are made aware that their social status will be based on their educational achievement, and thus study intensely (Vaughn, 1996). Attending cram schools after regular school every day is now a normative behavior among Japanese students. The children give up their "pastime of childhood for the all-consuming competition to get into a 'good' university" (Naff, 1994, p. 30).

Japanese society has come to be known as gakureki shakai ("educational credential society") as it places a great emphasis on the prestige of one's educational level (Chen, 1996). The number of those who go on to college has been increasing annually. The school system functions as the determinant of social class in Japan (Naka, 1977) and is now a universal standard for defining achievement (Vogel, 1996). Although education is still the most certain path to success, today's Japanese youths have fewer opportunities than their fathers or grandfathers did in the past, as an enormous number of individuals compete for the same position (Vaughn, 1996). In Japan, a college degree is necessary to obtain a decent job as a white-collar worker (Naka, 1977). Consequently, there is a "national obsession with academic achievement, which is measured and validated by the prominence of the school one is admitted to (not just at university level but at each entry level from kindergarten on) . . . ." (Greenfield & Cocking, 1994, p. 264).

The transition to middle school is especially consequential in Japan because the quality of middle school, along with entrance exams, strongly determines a child's career path (Gjerde, 1996). Academic performance in middle school determines what a child will do and be afterward. More than 65% of middle school students ranked average or above go to high school, whereas more than 65% of those ranked lowest do not (Harada, 1992). The delinquency level is significantly higher among those who perform poorly at school (Wagatsuma & De Vos, 1984), while 78.3% of the students who are ranked at least average academically do not have any delinquent history while in middle school (Harada, 1992).

The most drastic change happens from the last year of elementary school to the first year of middle school. Many children experience a great decline in their grades in these years (Yonezato, 1991). Teachers in middle school submit a report about a child, called naishinsho ("insider report about students"), to the high school where the child wishes to enter (Boys with Knives, 1997). Naishinsho contains the information on the students' life both at school and home. Since high schools regard naishinsho as very important when selecting candidates, middle school students must not only study hard but also be "good" at home and in the local community. Middle school students are thus forced to behave all day long. Consequently, Japanese students are under tremendous stress from being watched all the time.

This system is another means to make society more homogeneous (Boys with Knives, 1997). The high school wants to ensure that the students entering the school will not disrupt classes, so the individual's need for the group is fostered in school (Wagatsuma & Rosett, 1986). The growth of individuality and individualism is restricted through "a cultural framework of mind, which is built on the notions of harmony and loyalty to the group" (Marfording, 1997, p. 444) as well as rigid and strict disciplinary regulations in school. Thus, the more similar the students are with others, the better they are regarded (Boys with Knives, 1997).

Nevertheless, more problems at school, including school refusal (tokokyohi), bullying, and violent behavior, have come to the attention of educators in Japan in recent years (Lanham & Garrick, 1996). Harada (1992) has found that most delinquents start their "career" while in middle school. Another study suggests that juvenile delinquents experienced maladjustment to school first in middle school, mostly in the very first year (Suzuki, 1991). Delinquents evaluate school negatively and blame friendship (47.9%), grades (37.1%), and teachers (24.3%) for their delinquency (Suzuki, 1991). As delinquency levels increase, more students say that rigid school rules are the reasons for their maladjustment and delinquency. When coping with school problems, they mostly struggle with it alone (56.6%), take it out on parents (34.5%), or give up studying (28.5%) and go against teachers.

The Ministry of Education applied the five-day school system in public schools in the hope to reduce the pressure on today's children, but the consequence is that children are sent to additional cram school sessions (Naff, 1994). Also, teachers say that they cram a six-day curriculum into the five-day weeks (White, 1996). In addition, delinquent students have more opportunity to stay outside late at night and participate in problem behaviors (Hoshino et al., 1995).

When asked their academic level, the majority of delinquents answer that it is among the lowest in class (Harada, 1992; Yonezato, 1991). When the relationship between time to start delinquency and academic failure are divided into three groups–failure before delinquency, delinquency before failure, and simultaneous occurrence of failure and delinquency–the majority fall in the first group, suggesting that academic failure typically precedes delinquency.

### Peer Factors

Delinquent middle school students often claim friendship as a main cause of delinquency. Acceptance by peers and delinquency are, in fact, closely related (Yonezato, 1992). Those with high delinquency rates especially tend to blame their peers for their criminal acts (Semin &

Manstead, 1983). Moreover, those who blame others show less effort to disassociate with deviant peers (Kobayashi, 1989).

The way delinquents associate with their peers at school is different from that of nondelinquents (Uchiyama & Inokuchi, 1995). Regardless of delinquency level, almost all children engage in physical fights when they are in elementary school, but only delinquents continue doing so in middle school. Also, compared to nondelinquents, delinquent students are less likely to associate with those of the opposite sex, to study with peers, or to encourage friendship (Uchiyama & Inokuchi, 1995). Delinquent youths tend to associate with those who are antisocial and academically unsuccessful (Yonezato, 1992). During their free time, they mostly meet with peers at parks, streets, or open places (Suzuki et al., 1995).

Sixty-three percent of the delinquents in a survey reported feeling joyful when they are with their peers (Suzuki et al., 1995). They say that friends listen, give advice, and understand them. At the same time, many of them also admit to feeling stronger, as if they can do anything, when they are with peers. They tend to engage in much more delinquent behavior when in groups than alone. Also, they do such behaviors more often with the same peers than with other peers. Many of them have committed crimes impulsively as they loiter in the town with peers, seeking excitement. For example, many hotrodders in bosozoku say that they would not hotrod on the streets if they were alone (Tamura, 1989).

Group delinquency, more than one youth committing delinquent acts together, has been a major characteristic of juvenile crime. In Japan, however, the proportion of group delinquency has decreased since 1985 (Research and Training Institute Ministry of Justice, 1997). The percentage of group and individual delinquency was about 50% each in 1997 (Ministry of Justice, 1997). Of those who were arrested with peers, 44.7% were middle school students, 31.0% were high school students, 10% were juveniles who were employed, and the rest were juveniles who were unemployed (Suzuki et al., 1995).

Another significant peer factor related to delinquency is bullying, or ijime. The vast majority of delinquents have had an experience of ijime as a bully or victim or both (Sato, 1997b; Uchiyama & Inokuchi, 1995). The rate is higher among delinquents than nondelinquents. Ijime in Japan is believed to increase school violence, family violence, and juvenile delinquency (Ishikawa et al., 1991). Social ostracism, called nakama hazure, which means to be an "outsider" even within a group (Duke, 1986), is an important component of ijime in Japan, for one's self-identity is determined by his or her group membership and group identity (Lanham & Garrick, 1996). Overall, the number of ijime-related problems reported to the police increased from 95 in 1991 to 160 in 1995.

A victim seldom retaliates against his or her aggressor because the aggressor is his or her classmate and "friend," and the victim is somewhat dependent on the aggressor. To be bullied is better than to be alone for a child at this age. Furthermore, some cultural values of Japan contribute to the hesitance among children to report ijime to adult authority (Lanham, 1979). Some examples are the endurance of pain and hardship in silence, as well as the reluctance to object to one's group. In addition, there is a cultural tendency that the victim in ijime is often considered to be responsible for provoking the antagonist. Hence, ijime is often allowed to develop and persist. Those who are different often become targets of ijime (Lanham & Garrick, 1996; Sato, 1997b).

## CONCLUSION

These changes in family, school, and peer factors are related to the changes we see in juvenile delinquency since 1970. With fewer siblings, children spend more time by themselves, and when there is a single parent or both parents work, youth are often unsupervised. With an increase in family dysfunction, including child abuse, youth report wanting to spend more time with older youths, rather than with their parents and feel joyful when they are with their peers.

The extraordinary pressure to do well in school is a source of much stress and, often accompanied with bullying, has led to the phenomenon of many students refusing to go to school. Others go to school and engage in bullying because they do not want to be ostracized from their group.

Students who are unsuccessful in school or antisocial tend to associate with each other and to maintain the same peer group. Delinquents, especially those with the highest delinquency rates, attribute their behavior to their association with their peers and, indeed, do engage in more delinquent acts when they are with their peers. Changes in Japanese culture since 1979 have created an increase in problems in the family and school, and thereby increased the prominence of peers in the lives of youth.

Juvenile delinquency is a social and cultural phenomenon. Juvenile delinquency might be considered a plea of children. Through it, they may be pointing out that there is something wrong with the social environment in which we all live. The changes in cultural norms and values, the increase in anonymity and impersonality, the emergence of pseudo-reality and the corruption in youth culture are all manifestation of unhealthy changes in our society. Therefore, delinquency should be considered within this social context. Only then can we find a way to address these social problems, including juvenile delinquency.

## REFERENCES

Ames, W. (1981). *Police and community in Japan.* Berkeley, CA: University of California.

Azuma, H. (1994). *Two modes of cognitive socialization in Japan and the United States: Cross-cultural roots of minority child development.* Hillside, NJ: Lawrence Erlbaum.

Bayley, D. H. (1976a). Learning about crime: The Japanese experience. *Public Interest,* Summer, 68.

Bayley, D. H. (1976b). *Forces of order: Police behavior in Japan and the United States.* Berkeley: University of California.

Bayley, D. H. (1991). *Forces of order: Policing modern Japan.* Berkeley: University of California.

Befu, H. (1971). *Japan: An anthropological introduction.* San Francisco: Chandler.

Bell, R. (1971). *Social deviance.* Homewood, IL: Dorsey.

Bertrand, A. (1972). *Social organization.* Philadelphia: F. A. Davis.

Boys with Knives. (1997, April 30). Think or die [WWW document]. URL: *http://home3.highway.ne.jp/masada/english/knives.htm*

Burks, A. (1981). *Japan: Profile of a post industrial power.* Boulder: Westview.

Chen, S. (1996). Are Japanese young children among the gods? In D. W. Shwalb & B. J. Shwalb (Eds.), *Japanese childrearing: Two generations of scholarship* (pp. 31-43). New York: Guilford.

CIA. (2001). CIA The World Factbook 2001 [WWW document]. URL: *http://www.cia.gov/cia/publications/factbook/geos/ja.html*

Clifford, W. (1976). *Crime control in Japan.* Lexington, MA: Lexington.

Corrections Bureau. (1982). *Corrections institutions in Japan.* Tokyo: Ministry of Justice.

Duke, B. (1986). *The Japanese school.* New York: Praeger.

Forbis, W. H. (1975). *Japan today: People, places.* New York: Harper & Row.

Friedman, L. M. (1984). *American law: An introduction.* New York: Norton.

Gjerde, P. F. (1996). Longitudinal research in a cultural context: Reflections, prospects, challenges. In D. W. Shwalb & B. J. Shwalb (Eds.), *Japanese childrearing: Two generations of scholarship* (pp. 279-299). New York: Guilford.

Greenfield, P. M., & Cocking, R. R. (Eds.). (1994). *Cross-cultural roots of minority child development.* Hillside, NJ: Lawrence Erlbaum.

Hara, H., & Minagawa, M. (1996). From productive dependents to precious guests: Historical change in Japanese children. In D. W. Shwalb & B. J. Shwalb (Eds.),

*Japanese childrearing: Two generations of scholarship* (pp. 9-26). New York: Guilford.

Harada, Y. (1992). A retrospective study on the relationship of delinquent history in junior high school to later school and employment careers. *Reports of the National Research Institute of Police Science, 33*, 1-13.

Hata, H., & Smith, W. A. (1983). The vertical structure of Japanese society as a utopia. *Review of Japanese Culture and Society, 1*, 92-109.

Hoshino, K., Suzuki, S., Inokuchi, Y., Watanabe, K., & Suzuki, M. (1995). A study on the impact of introducing five day school week upon the life style of students and delinquents: Attitude of juveniles towards community programs for preventing delinquency one and a half years after the introduction. *Reports of the National Research Institute of Police Science, 36*, 1-17.

Inoue, T. (1977). The structure of seken-tei (appearances). *Review of Japanese Culture and Society, 1*, 51-61.

Ishikawa, E., Ito, S., Shimomura, T., & Sekine, M. (1991). Ijime no hoteki mondai to gakko, katei. *Jurisuto, 976* (April), 15-41.

Kato, H. (1977). Characteristics of theories of Japanese culture. *Review of Japanese Culture and Society, 1*, 62-71.

Kawasaki, K. (1994). *Information and contemporary Japanese culture.* Tokyo: Tokyo University.

Kawasaki, K., & Haga, M. (1995). Urban youth culture in contemporary Japan: The individualism of Japanese youth. In K. Kawasaki & M. Haga (Eds.), *Toshisenen no ishikito kodo [Conscience and behavior of urban youth]* (pp. 213-227). Tokyo: Koseisha-kosekaku.

Kobayashi, J. (1989). A study on attribution of responsibility for delinquency: Juveniles' attribution of responsibility for delinquency of their own and others. *Reports of the National Research Institute of Police Science, 30*, 51-67.

Kondo, D. K. (1990). *Crafting selves: Power, gender, and discourses of identity in a Japanese workplace.* Chicago: University of Chicago.

Koseisho. (1998, October 8). Goiken boshu: Shoshika mondai [Opinions wanted: The low birthrate problem] [WWW document]. URL: *http://www.mhw.go.jp/iken/index.html*

Koyama, T. (1973). *Gendai shakaino oyakokankei: Shitsukeno shakaigakuteki bunseki [The contemporary relationship between parents and children: Sociological analysis of discipline].* Tokyo: Baifukan.

Kumagai, F. (1995). Families in Japan: Beliefs and realities. *Journal of Comparative Family Studies, 26*(1), 135-163.

Lanham, B. (1979). Ethics and moral precepts taught in schools of Japan and the United States. *Ethos, 7*(1), 1-8.

Lanham, B. B., & Garrick, R. J. (1996). Adult to child in Japan: Interaction and relations. In D. W. Shwalb & B. J. Shwalb (Eds.), *Japanese childrearing: Two generations of scholarship* (pp. 97-124). New York: Guilford.

Masatsugu, M. (1982). *The modern samurai society: Duty and dependence in contemporary Japan.* New York: American Management Associations.

Matsumoto, Y., Kamahara, K., Shirai, T., & Katsura, E. (1978). Resistance in prisoners to group psychotherapy. In National Criminal Justice Reference Service (Ed.), *In-*

*ternational summaries* (Vol. 2). (K. Nishimoto, Trans.) (pp. 65-74). Washington, DC: USGPO.

Naff, C. (1994). *About face: How I stumbled onto Japan's social revolution*. New York: Kodansha International.

Naka, H. (1977). *Japanese youth in a changing society*. (L. A. Bester & S. Amano, Trans.). Tokyo: The International Society for Educational Information..

Nakane, C. (1978). *Tateshakai no rikigaku [Dynamics of vertical society]*. Tokyo: Kodansha.

Orenstein, P. (July 1, 2001). *Parasites in preta porter are threatening Japan's economy*. New York Times.

Regoli, R. M., & Hewitt, J. D. (1997). *Delinquency in society* (3rd ed.). New York: McGraw-Hill.

Reischauer, E. O. (1988). *The Japanese today*. Cambridge, MA: Harvard University.

Research and Training Institute Ministry of Justice. (1997, October 30). The White Paper on Crime 1997 [WWW document]. URL: *http://www.moj.go.jp*

Sato, S. (1997a). Shinriteki gaisho to hiko tono kanren. *Hanzaishinrigaku Kenkyu, 35* (special edition), 90-92.

Sato, S. (1997b). Ijime ijimerare experience and juvenile delinquent. *Japan Journal of Criminal Psychology, 35*(1), 23-35.

Savells, J. (1991). Juvenile delinquency in Japan. *International Journal of Adolescence and Youth, 3*(1-2), 129-135.

Semin, G. R., & Manstead, A. S. R. (1983). *The accountability of conduct: A social psychological analysis*. London: Academic.

Shindo, H., Sato, N., Yuma, Y., Yasuda, K., & Oba, R. (1993). Hishakai hikoshonen no kotoshitsu ni kansuru kenkyu. *Homusogokenkyujo Kenkyubukiyo, 36*, 157-183.

Suzuki, S. (1991). Junior high school students' maladjustments in their family and school life and their parents' dealing with them. *Reports of the National Research Institute of Police Science, 32*, 36 45.

Suzuki, S., Inokuchi, Y., Watanabe, K., Kobayashi, J., Okeda, S., & Takahashi, Y. (1995). A study of juvenile co-offending: An analysis of companionship by offense type. *Reports of the National Research Institute of Police Science, 36*, 47-64.

Suzuki, Y. (1979). Dispositional decision-making in the criminal justice process: Objectives, discretion and guidelines. *UNAFEI Resource Materials Series, 16*, 184-196.

Takahashi, Y., & Kobayashi, J. (1989). Conditions provoking violence among junior high school students. *Reports of the National Research Institute of Police Science, 30*, 68-73.

Tamura, M. (1989). Changes in hotrodders in the past fifteen years: Recent problems and the countermeasures. *Reports of the National Research Institute of Police Science, 30*, 74-85.

Tanaka, M. (1986). Maternal authority in the Japanese family. In G. A. De Vos & T. Sofue (Eds.), *Religion and the family in East Asia* (pp. 227-36). Berkeley, CA: University of California.

Tanizawa, T. (1979). Sentencing standards in Japan. *UNAFEI Resource Materials Series, 16*, 197-221.

Triandis, H. C., Kagitcibasi, C., Choi, S. C., & Yoon, G. (Eds.). (1989). *Individualism and collectivism: Theory, research, and applications.* Thousand Oaks, CA: Sage.

Tronick, E. Z., Morelli, G. A., & Ivey, P. K. (1992). The Efe forager infant and toddler's pattern of social relationships: Multiple and simultaneous. *Developmental Psychology, 28,* 568-577.

Uchiyama, J., & Inokuchi, Y. (1995). An analysis of the relationship between daily life experiences and delinquency among junior high school students. *Reports of the National Research Institute of Police Science, 36,* 98-109.

Vago, S. (1988). *Law and society.* Englewood Cliffs, NJ: Prentice-Hall.

Vaughn, C. A. (1996). Socialization and school adaptation: On the lifework of George De Vos. In D. W. Shwalb & B. J. Shwalb (Eds.), *Japanese childrearing: Two generations of scholarship* (pp. 85-96). New York: Guilford.

Vogel, S. H. (1996). Urban middle-class Japanese family life, 1958-1996: A personal and evolving perspective. In D. W. Shwalb & B. J. Shwalb (Eds.), *Japanese childrearing: Two generations of scholarship* (pp. 177-200). New York: Guilford.

Wagatsuma, H., & De Vos, G. A. (1984). *Heritage of endurance.* Berkeley, CA: University of California.

Wagatsuma, H., & Rosett, A. (1986). The implications of apology: Law and culture in Japan and the United States. *Law and Society Review, 20,* 461-507.

Watanabe, K., Tamura, M., & Kurusu, H. (1995). Characteristics of juvenile homicide cases: Differences by offender-victim relationships. *Reports of the National Research Institute of Police Science, 36,* 18-29.

Westermann, T. D., & Burfeind, J. W. (1991). *Crime and justice in two societies: Japan and the United States.* Pacific Grove, CA: Brooks/Cole.

White, M. (1996). Renewing the new middle class: Japan's next families. In D. W. Shwalb & B. J. Shwalb (Eds.), *Japanese childrearing: Two generations of scholarship* (pp. 208-219). New York: Guilford.

The Word of Children. (1997, April 30). Think or die [WWW document]. URL: *http://home3.highway.ne.jp/masada/english/fridaye.htm*

Yamaguchi, S. (1990). *Personal and impersonal comparison: Accurate self-evaluation and maintenance of self-esteem.* Paper presented at the meeting of the 10th Japanese Group.

Yamaguchi, S. (1994). Collectivism among the Japanese: A perspective from the self. In U. Kim, H. C. Triandis, C. Kagitcibasi, S. C. Choi, & G. Yoon (Eds.), *Individualism and collectivism: Theory, research, and applications.* (pp. 175-188). Thousand Oaks, CA: Sage.

Yonezato, S. (1991). A study on the relations of the school achievement to juvenile delinquency: An analysis on the school achievement of delinquents by grade. *Reports of the National Research Institute of Police Science, 32,* 63-76.

Yonezato, S. (1992). A study on the relation of the school achievement to juvenile delinquency: An analysis of the self-concept and the peers. *Reports of the National Research Institute of Police Science, 33,* 62-69.

# Vietnamese Youth Gangs in Honolulu

Nghi Dong Thai

*University of Hawaii at Manoa*

**SUMMARY.** Traditional theories of the connection between immigrant youth and gangs have not been sufficient in explaining why some are not in gangs. Therefore, this study examines Vietnamese youth gangs in Honolulu and the factors contributing to Vietnamese delinquency and youth gang participation. Twenty-six interviews were conducted with agency, school, police, Vietnamese adults, and Vietnamese youth. Results suggest that though the content of the delinquency model is different for immigrant and nonimmigrant youth, the process is the same. Problems in the home, school, or neighborhood facilitate contact with delinquent youth, and association with delinquent peers increases the likelihood for

Nghi Dong Thai, MA, is a doctoral graduate student in the Community & Culture Psychology program at the University of Hawaii-Manoa, and Research Assistant for the Kalihi Valley Collaborative Project. She has served as the Assistant Director of the Asian Community & Cultural Center, Program Reseacher for the Youth Violence Alternative Project, Project Assistant for the Nebraska Court Improvement Project, Research Assistant for the Center on Disability Studies, and as an AmeriCorps member. Currently, she serves as a Student Reviewer for the *American Journal of Community Psychology*. She has published on teen courts, interdisciplinary rural health training, and youth gangs.

Address correspondence to: Nghi DongThai, Center on Disability Studies, University of Hawaii-Manoa, 1776 University Avenue, UA4-6, Honolulu, HI 96822.

[Haworth co-indexing entry note]: "Vietnamese Youth Gangs in Honolulu." Thai, Nghi Dong. Co-published simultaneously in *Journal of Prevention & Intervention in the Community* (The Haworth Press, Inc.) Vol. 25, No. 2, 2003, pp. 47-64; and: *Culture, Peers, and Delinquency* (ed: Clifford R. O'Donnell) The Haworth Press, Inc., 2003, pp. 47-64. Single or multiple copies of this article are available for a fee from The Haworth Document Delivery Service [1-800-HAWORTH, 9:00 a.m. - 5:00 p.m. (EST). E-mail address: docdelivery@haworthpress.com].

10.1300/J005v25n02_04

delinquency and gang involvement. Therefore, participation in youth gangs depends on peer relationships. This finding is congruent with the perceptions of youth, while adults appear less aware of the effects of peer relationships among youth. *[Article copies available for a fee from The Haworth Document Delivery Service: 1-800-HAWORTH. E-mail address: <docdelivery@haworthpress.com> Website: <http://www.HaworthPress. com>* © 2003 by The Haworth Press, Inc. All rights reserved.]

**KEYWORDS.** Vietnamese, gangs, delinquency, peers, community, culture

The Vietnamese who immigrated to the United States have changed and adapted in several ways. As they adjust to their new lives, the values and traditions of the past continue to be important to the Vietnamese people. They struggle to determine which parts of their culture they will retain and which parts they must abandon. For the children of these first generation immigrants and refugees, life is very different compared to their parents. They face new challenges and obstacles as they try to adapt (Thai, 1999; Zhou, 1997). Problems of having to straddle between two worlds may cause youth to lose connection to their family. For some, multiple challenges of school failure, cultural conflicts, unattainable personal aspirations, racism, family breakdown, and poverty have left few choices (Do, 1999; Zhou & Bankston, 1998). Though many Vietnamese youth do not have problems with adjusting to life in America, for others, these problems have made them turn towards delinquency and gangs as an alternative (Do, 1999; Martinez & Lee, 2000; Vigil & Yun, 1990; Zhou & Bankston, 1998). The central question then becomes why some Vietnamese youth become involved in delinquency and gangs while others do not.

Currently, there is no clear definition for gangs, with each locality and agency having a definition that fits their own purposes and needs (Spergel, 1995). The definition determines how gangs are counted and the seriousness of gang behavior (Binder, Geis, & Bruce, 1997). The problem with definitions is that "youth groups," "youth gangs" and "organized adult gangs" are not always clearly defined. The term gangs in the Asian-American context has been particularly confusing because different sources tend to use the term Asian gangs to refer to both loosely structured youth gangs and highly organized criminal groups. Though some Vietnamese youth have connections with members of organized crime, these relationships are infrequent. Thus, there is a danger to using the term Asian gang because it gives the incorrect impression that all Asian delinquents are involved with organized crime groups (Vigil & Yun, 1990). The Vietnamese youth gangs do not fit the pattern of other Asian, African-American or Latino street gangs because of their different characteristics (Vigil & Yun, 1990).

Most Vietnamese gang members tend to be young males between the ages of 15 and 24 (Do, 1999; Vigil & Yun, 1990). Like other American gangs, younger members are recruited because they will be treated more leniently; older members stay for economic reasons (Toy, 1995). Most gang members are not successful in school, feel alienated from the larger society, and see few merits in working hard and achieving success in the conventional way (Do, 1999). These youth are described as at risk for violence because of their age, lower levels of education, and poverty. Furthermore, the neighborhoods they resettle in may be poverty stricken and expose them to more violence and hostility from the communities (Chen & True, 1994).

Vietnamese youth gangs are described as fluid because of their loose structure and organization. There is little or no role differentiation and no concerns over turf like other American youth gangs. Without restrictions on being in one gang, members are free to drift in and out of other gangs. Gang members are usually mobile and travel in groups of six or more, moving from state to state. Wherever they go, they have friends or family that can offer them a place to stay and they sometimes have a leader in the community who helps them with jobs (English, 1995; Gross, 1989). The structural and geographical fluidity of the youth gangs further hinders the attempts of law enforcement agencies to combat the problem (Vigil & Yun, 1990). Despite the fluidity, this does not diminish the intensity of the personal bonds formed within the gang, which becomes their adopted family (Do, 1999; Vigil & Yun, 1990).

Unlike their counterparts, Vietnamese youth gangs avoid gang symbols and wearing of colors so as to not draw attention. Some don't even have gang names and consider themselves as part of a group rather than a gang. When markers are used, they are discrete. One symbol is the common tattoo in the shape of a small V, composed of five dots, that is placed on inconspicuous parts of the body such as the webbing between fingers (Gross, 1989; Vigil & Yun, 1990). The five dots represent tinh, tien, tu, toi, and thu (love, money, prison, sin, and revenge). If they have tattoos, they generally are in the forms of tigers, dragons, and snakes (Do, 1999).

In addition, unlike organized crime groups and African-American and Latino street gangs that are involved with drug dealing for money (Spergel, 1995), the Vietnamese discourage drug use and dealing because of the high risk and money needed for start-up (Vigil & Yun, 1990). Joe (1994) found that, in general, Asians disapproved of drugs because it brings unwanted trouble and is destructive for their families.

Like earlier immigrant gangs, some Vietnamese youth formed groups or gangs to protect themselves from harassment and beatings by other youth (Do, 1999; Vigil & Yun, 1990). Toy (1995) suggests that for many Asian youth, being victimized acts as a main catalyst for joining gangs as they seek protection and revenge. Whether they are victimized by other Asian or ethnic groups, many youths believe Asian gangs to be the only source of seeking revenge. Given the lack of protection provided by schools, family, and police, youth believe that joining a gang is the only rational choice for security and protection. Other reasons for Vietnamese youth to join gangs are poverty and the desire to obtain money. For the Vietnamese gangs, money is obtained from home invasions (Do, 1999; Vigil & Yun, 1990). Most of their crimes target Vietnamese communities because the Vietnamese often tend to keep large amounts of cash and gold within their homes. The Vietnamese are also distrustful of the police and courts and fear retribution if they report the crime. Not speaking fluent English also keeps them from going to the police (Do, 1999; English, 1995; Vigil & Yun, 1990).

There are several theories that have been used to look at youthful crime in immigrant populations. Opportunity structure theories emphasize the material and social structures that shape the values and activities of groups in American society. When people are not given reasonable opportunities for gaining wealth and social status equally, they will take advantage of illegitimate opportunities. Immigrants, who initially settle in urban neighborhoods where they have limited economic opportunities, poor schools, squalid housing, and high crime rates, may turn to crime (Martinez & Lee, 2000). Martinez and Lee (2000) also suggest that noncriminal immigrant groups sometimes get "contaminated" by the criminal opportunities in their neighborhoods.

Another traditional theory is social disorganization. One type of disorganization that is relevant to immigrant communities is when solidarity is weakened as the young generation adopts the values of the new community rather than the traditional values of the parents' generation. Another type of disorganization occurs when values of the older generation are interpreted differently over time or rules are not enforced. This leads to social disharmony and control is weakened. Disorganized neighborhoods will be less likely to control the behavior of their inhabitants (Martinez & Lee, 2000; Spergel, 1995; Waters, 1999).

One theory focuses on the process of migration to explain the rate of youth crime. Based on the immigrant youth gang literature, Waters (1999) suggested that the migration process itself causes waves of juvenile delinquency to occur. Four factors were examined: demographics, social cohesion, socioeconomics, and social psychological variables. The number of young males in an immigrant group was, by far, the most important factor. In this theory, a large proportion of young males, occurring within the context of the loss of control of traditional culture as children of immigrants come into contact with American culture at school and in neighborhoods and experience intergenerational conflict with their parents, leads to a higher rate of youth crime. Further, this effect is increased when there are misinterpretations by law enforcement and immigrants leading to inaccurate attributions of each other's behavior.

While the opportunity structure, social disorganization, and immigration theories begin to look at some of the reasons as to why youth may be prone to join gangs, they do not explain why some immigrant youth do not join gangs. The explanations of problems such as poverty and school problems causing immigrant youth to join gangs does not explain why some Asian gang members are from suburban middle-class families and are extremely good students (Zhou, 1997). The immigration theory, with its focus on group rates, does not explain why many members in a large cohort of immigrant young males do not become involved in crime. In addition, the focus on the immigration process led Waters to state, "I must reluctantly conclude that little can be done to prevent outbreaks of youthful crime among immigrant populations" (Waters, 1999, p. 202).

An alternative to the traditional theories is that Vietnamese delinquency and youth gangs are similar to patterns of other youth. O'Donnell (1998, 2000) presented a model in which peer associations are a function of conditions in youth's homes, schools, and neighborhoods. Problems in homes and schools increase the likelihood of spending time outside of home and school with youth with similar problems, in settings lacking responsible adult supervision. Problem neighborhoods (easy access to drugs, guns, and criminal activities) provide opportunities for participation with other youth involved in these activities. In this model, peer relationships are the key link between the community (families, schools, and neighborhoods) and delinquency, including youth gangs. This model is supported by studies showing that involvement in youth gangs is strongly associated with peer associations (Short, 1996; Spergel, 1995), including some studies on Vietnamese gangs (Do, 1999; Toy, 1995; Zhou & Bankston, 1998).

From this perspective, immigration may affect community life in families, schools, and neighborhoods, but the key variable for immigrant youth is the same as for other youth, i.e., the effect of these community conditions on peer associations. Therefore, the importance of immigration is the effect on community life, rather than any direct effect on participation in delinquency or youth gangs.

Several studies support this alternative theory. Kent and Felkenes (1998) and Wyrick (2000) conducted focus groups and interviewed 232 youth gang members and their parents to look at the cultural and non-cultural reasons for joining gangs. Results showed that Vietnamese who reject Asian identity and find it difficult to adopt an American identity are not more likely than other Vietnamese youth to join youth gangs. The belief that youth gain an identity through gang involvement, when they can't find it from their family, was not supported. Instead, there were two main predictors of Vietnamese youth gang involvement: pro-gang attitudes and exposure to gangs in the neighborhood. In addition, there were four factors that influenced a pro-gang attitude: negative school attitude, family conflict, poor social integration (alienation), and perceived benefits of a gang. These studies suggest that Vietnamese youth gangs are related to being exposed to gangs or associating with delinquent peers, while negative school attitude and family conflict may serve to increase contact with delinquent peers. Kim and Goto (2000) found that even among Asian-American adolescents, a majority of whom were second-generation youth, who did not have any difficulty with their parents due to cultural values, the strongest predictor of delinquency was high association with other delinquent peers.

Studies on Vietnamese delinquency and youth gangs in Hawaii are nonexistent. Therefore, the goal of this study is to increase understanding of Vietnamese delinquency and youth gangs in Honolulu. Specifically, the main issue to be addressed is the role of immigration in Vietnamese delinquency and participation in youth gangs.

## *METHOD*

Data for this study were collected from 26 open-ended ethnographic interviews with representatives from community agencies in Honolulu, the Honolulu Police Department, Honolulu schools, and Vietnamese adults and youth living in Honolulu. The interviews were conducted September through December 2001. Six interviews were conducted with individuals from different agencies in the community that provide services for Vietnamese youth and immigrants and a program that works with youth gangs. The interviewees were people knowledgeable about their Vietnamese clients and consisted of three program directors, a case manager, a community health worker, and a clinical psychologist.

Two interviews were conducted with police officers at the Honolulu Police Department. One officer was a detective working in the Juvenile Services Division's Gang Awareness Detail and the other was a detective in the Criminal Investigation Division. Both were regarded as the most knowledgeable on Vietnamese gangs and youth gangs in general.

Seven representatives from schools with the highest proportion of Vietnamese students were also interviewed. The interviewees from the schools consisted of three English-as-a-Second Language Learner (ESLL) coordinators, one regular counselor, one outreach counselor, and two part-time ESLL teachers. The interviewees for the agencies, schools, and police were ethnically diverse. They included four people of Japanese descent, three Caucasians, one Hawaiian-Chinese, two Chinese, three Vietnamese, one Filipino, and one unknown.

The Vietnamese adults and youth were located by means of the snowball technique. The Vietnamese adults were recruited from one of the agencies and from the school interviewees. Six interviews were conducted with Vietnamese adults. There were three males and three females and their ages ranged from 29-60 years old. Two were unemployed due to health reasons and another for a disability. One was unemployed but in nail school. The other three Vietnamese adults consisted of a part-time ESLL teacher, a student at the University of Hawaii, and a writer for the Vietnamese newspaper. One of the six Vietnamese adults obtained a four-year degree in the United States from the University of Hawaii and was taking additional classes to be a teacher. The others, educated in Vietnam, included one who had a master's degree and was a university professor, one who was a teacher, one who was a high school graduate, one who never went to school, and one whose education was unknown. All were born in Vietnam. The amount of time they lived in the United States varied for each individual. One person had been in Hawaii for 4 months, two for almost 3 years, one for 6 years, and two for 11-12 years.

One group interview consisting of two youth and five individual interviews were conducted with Vietnamese youth, three males and four females born in Vietnam, referred by the ESLL coordinators. Five of the youth were 18, one was 17, and one was 16 years old. Five of the students were seniors in high school and the other two were juniors. Two of the youth had part-time jobs. The amount of time they lived in the

United States ranged from 4 months at the time of the interview to 11 years. Three had been in the United States for less than two-and-one-half years and the other four had been in the United States for at least seven years.

Informed consent was obtained from all participants prior to interviewing and parental consent was obtained before interviewing youth under 18. Consent forms were available in both English and Vietnamese. The interviews ranged from 10-60 minutes with the majority averaging 30 minutes. Topics and prompts were carefully chosen for each group that was interviewed. Specific questions for each group covered the agencies, social services available for Vietnamese clients, information about the schools, HPD programs, police tracking, etc. Topics for all interviews covered information about the Vietnamese, their families, neighborhoods they live in, the schools they go to, the youth, problems or issues they are dealing with, and perceptions of Vietnamese delinquency and youth gangs. All 26 interviews were audio recorded and transcribed verbatim. Twenty of the interviews were conducted in English while six were in Vietnamese.

Information from the interviews was also collected on contextual factors such as demographic patterns of the Vietnamese immigrants, the history of Vietnamese immigrants in Hawaii, and the law enforcement/legal system in Hawaii to understand the context-specific and community level factors for Vietnamese delinquency and youth gangs. Information on the Vietnamese population in Hawaii was obtained through the United States Census Bureau. An extensive search of the major newspapers, the *Honolulu Star-Bulletin* and the *Honolulu Advertiser*, through the Internet and local newspaper index of the state libraries was also conducted for articles relating to Vietnamese immigrants and refugees and any problems with Vietnamese youth gangs or crime. In addition, statistics on juvenile arrests for Vietnamese youth were gathered from the Juvenile Justice Information System (JJIS), a subdivision within the Hawaii State Department of the Attorney General. The purpose of the JJIS is to create and maintain a juvenile crime database for the State of Hawaii. Information is received from the police, family courts, prosecutors, and the Hawaii Youth Correctional Facility.

The interviews were read multiple times and coded initially by hand. The passages coded were related primarily to information involving Vietnamese delinquency and youth gangs. The transcribed interviews were imported to the QSR NVivo program (a computer program for qualitative data) and coded again in the program with the hand coding used as a guide for comparison and consistency. The themes or abstract constructs (Ryan & Bernard, 2002) that emerged from the analysis were considered in relation to the research questions. Comparisons were made between the representatives of agencies, schools, police, and Vietnamese adults to look at similarities and differences in the perception of youth gangs. Comparisons were also made between Vietnamese youth gangs in Honolulu and research studies on Vietnamese youth gangs on the Mainland.

## RESULTS

Results from this study are presented first with a brief overview of the Vietnamese in Hawaii followed by the presence of youth gangs on school campuses. Following this, gangs in Hawaii and how the police track them are examined. In addition, arrest statistics for Vietnamese youth from the JJIS are presented. Finally, the reasons why Vietnamese youth are becoming delinquent or involved in gangs is examined followed by a comparison of the Vietnamese youth gangs in Honolulu, Hawaii, to the ones on the Mainland. In addition, 10 of the 26 interviewees did not specifically speak about or have knowledge about Vietnamese youth gangs. Therefore, though their interviews were included in the results section, they were not always counted in parts of the section on the reasons Vietnamese youth join gangs or on the characteristics of Vietnamese youth gangs.

Currently, there are 7,867 Vietnamese living in Hawaii (U.S. Bureau of the Census, 2000). They include refugees, immigrants, and an emerging second generation that includes ethnic Vietnamese, Chinese-Vietnamese, and Amerasians. According to the school interviewees, the number of Vietnamese students was much higher in the past, but most have graduated and there are now only between 10-30 at each school.

Though the youth at these schools interact well now, problems between ethnic groups and with gangs seemed to be prevalent in the past on school campuses. These conflicts appeared to occur at a time when an influx of newer Vietnamese immigrants came into the Hawaii school system in the early 1990s. As reported by several interviewees (N = 6), there are currently gang members or gangs on several of these campuses, but no gang-related problems on campus. According to a few school interviewees (N = 2), the campus atmosphere appears to be safer now and this has much to do with Chapter 19, the school rules and guidelines system, at all of the public schools. Each school has a different referral system for youth who get into trouble, but most follow

Chapter 19 in which violations are broken down into different areas and strictly enforced, resulting in detention, in-school suspension, or sus-pension.

Police maintain a computer database system. When police officers come into contact with a person who meets the criteria of being in a gang, they document the information that is later entered into the data-base. While some gang members are encountered on the street, others may be identified in school through the referral of a counselor.

The definition of a gang used by the police takes into consideration four criteria: (1) a gang must have a name, (2) a gang must have three or more members who meet on a continual basis with the exclusion of other groups, (3) gangs may claim turf, and (4) a gang engages in crimi-nal behavior. Gang membership is broken down into four levels. First, there are the hard-core members who make up the nucleus of the gang. They're the ones who would commit a murder in the name of the gang and most often run into trouble with the law. Then there are the active members who will commit crimes for the gang. The general members are initiated into the gang, but are on reserve status, so when there is a problem, they are called to help. There are also the associate members who have not been initiated into the gang, but hang out with the gang.

To be a gang member, the database system uses several criteria. These include admitting that one is in a gang, having tattoos that show gang association, dressing consistently as a gang member, attending gang activities, using symbols or hand signs related to gangs, associat-ing with recognized gang members, possessing gang paraphernalia, having prior arrests with gang members, committing crimes consistent with gang activity, and being identified by other gang members, family members, law enforcement officers, or a reliable informant. Though in-volvement with criminal activities is not always necessary to be identi-fied as a gang member, any 3 of the 12 criteria will classify youth as a gang member.

JJIS statistics showed that the age range for Vietnamese youth who were arrested January 1999 through February 2002 is 7-17 years old. There were a total of 158 youth arrested, 95 males and 63 females. The types of offenses include assault, truancy, possession of drugs, bur-glary, and running away from home, with no obvious signs of offenses related to gang involvement. The high numbers of runaway and truant youth may reflect problems in the home.

Though the majority of the Vietnamese adapt well and are successful, there are others with serious problems. It was perceived by the interviewe-es that the youth were becoming delinquent or joining gangs because of a myriad of problems they were facing in their home, neighborhood, and school contexts. Interestingly, there were youth who did have a problem in many spheres of their lives, but were not involved in delinquency or youth gangs, while there were also youth who had stable families and were excellent students, but were still involved in gangs.

Undoubtedly, one of the major challenges facing Vietnamese families as perceived by the interviewees was the generation gap between parents and children. Many ($N = 13$) spoke about how hard it was for parents to understand why their children have changed, while their children do not understand why the parents still adhere to the traditional ways. These differences in expectations and values as the children become more acculturated to their new environment can cause a culture conflict to occur within families.

Interviewees ($N = 9$) also saw communication within families as a major issue for some as the children become increasingly more Americanized and lose the Vietnamese language. Several interviewees mentioned how it becomes difficult for parents to communicate with their children as they are not fluent in English and the children are not fluent in Vietnamese. The children may also feel ashamed that their parents do not speak English. This lack of communication and disrespect for parents was seen as another reason contributing to instability in the Vietnamese family.

Interestingly, even though a majority of the adult and agency interviewees ($N = 13$) blamed the family and home life above all other reasons for the causes of Vietnamese delinquency and youth gangs, it was attributed more to the fact that Vietnamese parents worked too much and therefore could not supervise or spend time with their children, than to reasons relating to the generation gap, communication barriers, or conflict between American and Vietnamese ways. Further, interviewees saw that it was this lack of supervision and support of their children that caused the youth to turn towards their friends. This lack of supervision or support in the family environment was believed to be an important factor causing Vietnamese youth to turn towards their peers and eventually get involved in gangs.

About half of the adult interviewees ($N = 10$) mentioned that the Vietnamese students, newcomers and mainstream alike, were excellent students and leaders at their school. However, for those faring poorly in school but with pressures to excel from their parents, the school years can be more challenging and difficult. Feelings of alienation and the inability to ask for help from teachers at school or parents at home may lead to frustrations and a sense of hopelessness. The motivation to go to school decreases as they fall behind in school and fail classes. As a result of their school problems, the youth have a need to belong somewhere and so they start to hang out with other youth who have similar problems. Truancies become more common and many times the parents are not aware that this is going on. They may drop out and quit going to school altogether. These school problems were seen as factors contributing to Vietnamese youth becoming delinquent and joining gangs.

The idea that being in a gang was also based on ethnicity was supported by other interviewees (N = 3). One ESLL coordinator mentioned that though most of the gang problems on his campus in the early 1990s involved more mainstream youth, the newcomer youth were pulled into the confrontations because they were Vietnamese.

Several of the interviewees (N = 8) perceived that the freedom offered in the United States was a problem for youth. With too much spare time after school, the kids had the opportunity to get involved in negative activities such as using drugs, smoking cigarettes, and fighting. According to several interviewees (N = 7), too much freedom can lead to more serious consequences for some. When their children get involved in negative behaviors, the parents may punish them and some types of punishment are perceived as child abuse to outsiders. Issues around abuse seemed to deal with a misunderstanding of the Vietnamese culture from the school and police perspective. They see Vietnamese parents who beat their children as abusive while Vietnamese parents see it as discipline or education. The result is that when the school, police or CPS get involved, this sends the message to Vietnamese parents that they should be careful with the type of punishment they use on their children or the law may take their children away. Knowing this, the children may feel they have more power in the families while the parents lose their authority to control their children who are now becoming too Americanized from the parents' perspective. Eventually, several interviewees (N = 10) felt that the freedom and lack of power that parents hold over their children cause Vietnamese youth to become uncontrollable and lead them down the wrong path.

Some interviewees (N = 7) believed it was the neighborhood in which the youth lived that caused them to join gangs. Particularly, this was seen to be true for youth from poor neighborhood areas. The concern with the neighborhoods appears to be more related to those living in the neighborhoods than the area itself. In other words, the Vietnamese kids in gangs initially grew up together and were friends with each other. If one person experienced a problem, they would come to each other's aid and eventually their group may turn into a gang. The presence of gangs in neighborhoods also provides the opportunity for other Vietnamese youth to join.

Another factor that seemed to contribute to youth joining gangs was the need for protection as mentioned by both adult (N = 8) and youth (N = 2) interviewees. According to the police, because the Vietnamese students tended to be smaller than their peers, they often were picked on by other youth from different ethnic groups. This would cause them to join a gang in order to get protection or revenge on the person who bothered them. The Vietnamese youth saw themselves more as a group of friends than a gang and, when somebody else was picking on one person, they would band together and protect each other. Fights could occur over girls, getting a bad look from someone, or simply by misunderstanding someone.

According to the police and one ESLL coordinator, money was also a key draw for some Vietnamese youth to join gangs. Wanting recognition and power, money can be an easy way to buy that image. In addition, the emphasis on material possessions in American culture increases the desire for money but youth want to earn it quickly instead of through the traditional ways of working.

Lastly, a majority of the interviewees (N = 12) also mentioned that the type of peers youth associated with could contribute to their delinquency or youth gang involvement. Particularly, all of the interviewees who mentioned that peers were a problem perceived that only youth with problems would eventually gravitate towards friends who have similar problems and "bad" youth may be more likely to hook up with the other problem kids.

No difference was found in perceptions of Vietnamese delinquency and youth gangs between agencies, the schools, police, or Vietnamese adults. However, perceptions of reasons for youth gang involvement differed for the adults and youth. Only the adult interviewees stressed problems such as families, environment, needing money, or having too much free time as reasons why youth joined gangs, while not one of the youth mentioned anything about those types of problems. Regarding problems at school, only adults mentioned academic problems at school to lead towards joining gangs. For youth, it seemed to only involve conflicts with other youth, not academic failure that would lead to gang involvement. In addition, sometimes youth felt that they were mistakenly labeled as gangs when they were only trying to protect themselves or friends. Particularly, none of the youth said anything about having problems with family as a reason for youth to join gangs, whereas for the adult interviewees, the family was the most mentioned reason for gang involvement.

In fact, two of the youth interviewed had poor relationships with their parents but neither of these youths were in gangs. Two different youths interviewed mentioned they did not spend much time with their parents. One male youth said he had a good relationship with his parents but did not spend much time with them. Despite his good relationship with his parents, this male interviewee had been involved with a youth gang and had to switch schools to leave the gang behind.

Vietnamese youth gang members are usually male and some start as early as intermediate school. Though Mainland Vietnamese youth gangs are described as fluid with little structure, the Vietnamese youth gangs in Hawaii were both described as tightly organized by some and as fluid by others. The police viewed Vietnamese youth gangs to be not cohesive and to have some structure with a leader. The Vietnamese youth gangs in Hawaii do not claim turf or territory. Both mainstream and newcomer youth have been known to join the Vietnamese youth gangs, though interestingly a majority of those described in gangs were the mainstream youth.

Further, like the Mainland Vietnamese gangs, money was a central focus for Vietnamese youth gangs in Hawaii. Many of them joined for money and would be involved in selling drugs, home invasions, or extortion. The police mentioned that sometimes gang members would mark up their bodies with scars to scare their victims into giving up their money. Other crimes they have been involved with are assaults, property damage, and graffiti. According to the police, the victims were often members of their own community.

A major difference between the Vietnamese youth gangs on the Mainland and in Hawaii also appears to be their involvement with drugs. Though gangs on the Mainland discourage drug use and dealing, drugs appear to be a big problem for the Vietnamese youth in Hawaii.

Vietnamese girls have also been known to join youth gangs on either an associate level or as girlfriends of gang members. Once in the gang, they are cared for by the other male gang members and may be looked upon as little sisters. It was perceived that girls who got involved with the youth gangs were ones who had problems with their family. Some become pregnant and run away from home, and may later be involved in prostitution or strip dancing.

Many of these youth begin to leave gangs as they get older, get married, have families, acquire jobs, or move away. Even though they may leave the gang, they don't leave completely. They still have loyalty to their gang and if someone needs help, they go to their aid. Interviewees from all five groups expressed that currently the presence of Vietnamese youth gangs is no longer as problematic as it used to be. With the stricter rules on school campuses and the fact that most have graduated from high school and moved away, the Vietnamese youth in gangs that are still around are described as "low-key."

## *DISCUSSION*

The central finding from this study suggests that the strongest factor for Vietnamese delinquency and youth gang participation is peer association. Specifically, immigrant youth become delinquent or join gangs in much the same process as nonimmigrant youth. That is, the problems with immigration such as culture conflict, the generation gap, and communication barriers between parents and youth becomes the content that can affect peer networks and lead to delinquency (O'Donnell, 1998, 2000). Nonimmigrant youth also have problems with family, school, or neighborhood that can lead to delinquency. Therefore, the process is the same for both immigrant and nonimmigrant youth: youth who have problems in their home, school, or neighborhood and have delinquent peers are more likely to become delinquent, whereas youth who have the same problems, but do not associate with delinquent peers, are not likely to become delinquent or to join gangs.

This central finding is supported by the difference in perception between adults and youth of why youth become delinquent or join gangs. While the agency, school, police, and Vietnamese adult interviewees mostly believed that Vietnamese youth were joining gangs due to problems with their family, neighborhoods, school, and peers, the youth had a very different perspective. The Vietnamese youth interviewees said that youth joined gangs, or were sometimes labeled as gangs, because of fights they had with other youth for protection or because they were picked on by others. Not one of the Vietnamese youth mentioned having problems with family or school as the reason either they or others they knew became involved with gangs. Therefore, the differences between the youth and adults suggest that the realities of perception vary according to context. While the agency, school, police, and Vietnamese adults perceive that problems in the school, home, or neighborhood context accounted for delinquency and youth gangs, the youth viewed it within the context of peer relationships.

Interestingly, many interviewees (N = 8) pointed toward the lack of parental supervision and support as being a problem, yet several (N = 4) of the Vietnamese youth interviewed, who were not in gangs, had parents who were not at home due to work. On the other hand, there were also those who have at least one parent at home or had parents who were very supportive and well-educated, but yet still were involved in delinquency or gangs. Some believed it was the environment that made a difference with those living in better neighborhoods not involved in gangs. Yet, several of the Vietnamese youth from poorer, high-crime neighborhoods were not in gangs, while some who were from better neighborhoods were involved in gangs. Some mentioned that the ones not in gangs are the good students who are motivated to learn, yet there were several examples of good students who were involved in gangs. Another misperception was that the youth who were not delinquent had various services available to them or were in positive activities. Yet, from those youth who were interviewed, the lack of structured activities in their lives did not mean that they were involved in gangs.

While association with delinquent peers seems to be key to youth gang involvement, the families, schools, and neighborhoods/communities can be pivotal in discouraging youth from delinquency. From the family perspective, parents can help to prevent delinquency by deterring their children from associating with delinquent friends. By being aware of the type of friends their children have and what activities they are involved in, parents can influence their children's choice of friends.

Prevention can be taken a step further by changing school policies and guidelines that put youth who get in trouble into contact with other delinquent youth. Policies that track youth by ability or bring youth together during detention or in-school suspension may actually be more harmful than helpful by strengthening their ties with youth with similar problems. This may also be true for youth who are suspended from school since they have increased chances for contact with other suspended youth. An alternative would be to provide volunteer duties or other programs where youth who get in trouble do not come into contact with other delinquent peers.

Prevention can also be undertaken in the neighborhoods and communities to keep youth from coming into contact with delinquent peers. In neighborhoods that have crime, positive programs can be developed so youth are supervised by responsible adults and meet youth who are not delinquent. If financially feasible, the family also can move out of the neighborhood to discourage contact with delinquent youth. In addition, suggestions for the Vietnamese community in general include services that try to bridge the gap between Vietnamese parents and their children and provide more opportunities for learning English.

A limitation to this study is that of the youth who were interviewed, only one had been involved in a youth gang. It would have been beneficial to have been able to recruit more youth who were in gangs to further understand their perspective.

## REFERENCES

Binder, A., Geis, G., & Bruce, D.D., Jr. (1997). *Juvenile delinquency: Historical, cultural, and legal perspectives.* Cincinnati, OH: Anderson Publishing.

Chen, S.A. & True, R.H. (1994). Asian/Pacific Island Americans. In L.D. Eron, J.H. Gentry & P. Schlegel (Eds.), *Reason to hope: A psychosocial perspective on violence and growth* (pp. 145-161). Washington, DC: American Psychological Association.

Do, H.D. (1999). *The Vietnamese Americans.* Westport, CT: Greenwood Press.

English, T.J. (1995). *Born to kill.* New York: William Morrow.

Gross, G. (1989). The Vietnamese crime network. In H.M. Launer & J.E. Palenski (Eds.), *Crime and the new immigrants* (pp. 33-39). Springfield, IL: Charles C. Thomas.

Joe, K.A. (1994). The new criminal conspiracy? Asian gangs and organized crime in San Francisco. *Journal of Research in Crime and Delinquency, 31*(4), 390-415.

Kent, D.R. & Felkenes, G.T. (1998). *Cultural explanations for Vietnamese youth gang involvement in street gangs* (No. 180955). Washington, DC: US Department of Justice, Office of Juvenile Justice and Delinquency Prevention. Retrieved February 12, 2001, from *http://www.ncjrs.org/pdffiles1/ojjdp/180955.pdf*

Kim, T.E. & Goto, S.G. (2000). Peer delinquency & parental social support as predictors of Asian American adolescent delinquency. *Deviant Behavior, 21,* 331-347.

Martinez, R. & Lee, M.T. (2000). On immigration and crime. *Criminal Justice, 1,* 485-524.

O'Donnell, C. R. (1998, May). *Peers and delinquency: Implications for prevention and intervention.* Presentation at the Violence and Youth: Overcoming the Odds: Helping Children and Families at Risk Conference, Miami, FL.

O'Donnell, C. R. (2000). *Youth with disabilities in the juvenile justice system: A literature review.* Clemson, SC: Consortium on Children, Families, and the Law, Clemson University, Institute on Family and Neighborhood Life.

Ryan, G.W. & Bernard, H.R. (2002). *Techniques to identify themes in qualitative data.* Retrieved February 4, 2002, from *http://www.analytictech.com/mb870/ryan-bernard_techniques_to_identify_themes_in.htm*

Short, J.F. (1996). *Gangs & adolescent violence.* Boulder, CO: Center for Study and Prevention of Violence.

Spergel, I.A. (1995). *The youth gang problem: A community approach.* New York: Oxford University Press.

Thai, H.C. (1999). Splitting things in half is so white!: Conceptions of family life and friendship and the formation of ethnic identity among second generation Vietnamese Americans. *Amerasia Journal, 25*(1), 53-88.

Toy, C. (1995). Coming out to play: Reasons to join and participate in Asian gangs. *The Gang Journal, 1,* 13-29.

U.S. Bureau of the Census (2000). *Population by race and Hispanic or Latino origin, for all ages and for 18 years and over, for Hawaii: 2000.* Retrieved October 3, 2001, from *http://www.census.gov/Press-Release/www/2001/tables/dp_hi_2000.xl*

Vigil, J.D. & Yun, S.C. (1990). Vietnamese youth gangs in southern California. In R. Huff (Ed.), *Gangs in America* (pp. 146-162). Newbury Park, CA: Sage.

Waters, T. (1999). *Crime and immigrant youth.* Thousand Oaks, CA: Sage.

Wyrick, P.A. (2000). *Vietnamese youth gang involvement* (Fact Sheet No. 200001). Washington, DC: U.S. Department of Justice, Office of Juvenile Justice and Delinquency Prevention.

Zhou, M. (1997). Growing up American: The challenge confronting immigrant children and children of immigrants. *Annual Review of Sociology, 23,* 63-95.

Zhou, M. & Bankston III, C.L. (1998). *Growing up American: How Vietnamese children adapt to life in the United States.* New York: Russell Sage.

# Juvenile Delinquency:
# Peer Influences, Gender Differences and Prevention

Renee J. Galbavy

*University of Hawaii at Manoa*

**SUMMARY.** Previous research exploring the formation and influence of peer relationships on male and female delinquency has found a strong connection between friendships with antisocial peers and involvement in delinquent activity. Although there has been a substantial amount of research exploring these relationships, the majority of studies have focused upon male adolescents. This qualitative study was designed to compare genders on the influence of peer relationships contributing to delinquent behavior. Information was obtained through interviews with 10 male and 10 female incarcerated juvenile offenders. The intent of the study was to seek support for the influence of peer relationships on fe-

Renee J. Galbavy, MA, is a Doctoral Candidate in the Community and Culture Psychology program at the University of Hawaii. She is certified in Disaster Management, Humanitarian Assistance and International Peacekeeping. She is presently a Psychology Instructor at Pennsyvania State University, New Kensington, and the Community College of Allegheny County. She is actively working on her dissertation "Influences on the Effectivness of Mentoring At-Risk Youth."

Address correspondence to: Renee J. Galbavy, Department of Psychology, University of Hawaii, 2430 Campus Road, Honolulu, HI 96822.

[Haworth co-indexing entry note]: "Juvenile Delinquency: Peer Influences, Gender Differences and Prevention." Galbavy, Renee J. Co-published simultaneously in *Journal of Prevention & Intervention in the Community* (The Haworth Press, Inc.) Vol. 25, No. 2, 2003, pp. 65-78; and: *Culture, Peers, and Delinquency* (ed: Clifford R. O'Donnell) The Haworth Press, Inc., 2003, pp. 65-78. Single or multiple copies of this article are available for a fee from The Haworth Document Delivery Service [1-800-HAWORTH, 9:00 a.m. - 5:00 p.m. (EST). E-mail address: docdelivery@haworthpress.com].

male delinquency. However, the data analysis revealed themes indicating that family functioning influences were more important for females. The themes for the male delinquents indicated that peer relationships had a strong influence on their behavior. Other themes for both males and females were related to school and their feelings regarding the consequences of their delinquent actions. *[Article copies available for a fee from The Haworth Document Delivery Service: 1-800-HAWORTH. E-mail address: <docdelivery@haworthpress.com> Website: <http://www.HaworthPress. com> © 2003 by The Haworth Press, Inc. All rights reserved.]*

**KEYWORDS.** Delinquency, peers, gender, community

The study of youth crime has spanned decades and taken many different forms. Although there still remain many unanswered questions concerning the most effective intervention for this behavior, research has indicated the most prevalent risks for delinquent behavior. These include: community/demographic, school, family functioning, peer and social influences, and individual level characteristics (Chung & Elias, 1996; Farrington, 1996; Henggeler, 1991; Lowry, Sleet, Duncan, Powell, & Kolbe, 1995; Mulvey & Woolard, 1997; Tolan, & Guerra, 1994). The most powerful risk for delinquency is gender (Giordano & Cernkovich, 1997; Leonard, 1982; Siegel & Senna, 1981). Gender is important because of the substantial differences in both the formation and seriousness of delinquent behavior in males and females.

To fully appreciate the importance of gender in the development of delinquent behavior, it is essential to look at the role it has taken over the years. Historically, males have committed the majority of juvenile crimes, including violent crimes such as murder, assault, robbery, and rape (Calhoun, Jurgens, & Chen, 1993; Giordano & Cernkovich, 1997; Heimer, 1996; Lowry et al., 1995; White & LaGrange, 1987). However, over the last couple of decades, female delinquents have exhibited increasing levels of aggressive behavior and violent criminal activity (Calhoun et al., 1993; Molidor, 1996; Pakiz, Reinherz, & Frost, 1992).

Adolescent female offenders have been largely ignored both in research on female delinquent behavior and in the development of intervention and educational programs (Fejes-Mendoza, Miller, & Eppler, 1995; Miller, Trapani, Fejes-Mendoza, Eggleston, & Dwiggins, 1995). The reason for this may be that for many years female adolescents were a comparatively small proportion of the known delinquent offenders. However, as the seriousness of female crime has increased, so has the number of female offenders (Snyder & Sickmund, 1999).

Peer groups and social networks provide both risk and protection and have a major effect on both female and male delinquent behavior (Cullingford & Morrison, 1997; Elliot & Menard, 1996; Farrington, 1996; Goldstein, 1990; O'Donnell, Manos, & Chesney-Lind, 1987; Thornberry & Krohn, 1997; Thornberry, Lizotte, Krohn, Farnworth, & Jang, 1994; Warr, 1993). The people a person spends time with determine with whom relationships develop. Studies of relationships and behavior have shown that the behavior of the peers is associated with the behavior of each individual (O'Donnell & Tharp, 1990).

Although there may be many reasons why delinquent youths enter antisocial peer groups (such as negative family environments, feelings of rejection, and school problems), the deviant peer relationship itself strongly impacts some individuals who commit criminal acts (Cullingford & Morrison, 1997; Elliot & Menard, 1996; Farrington, 1996; O'Donnell et al., 1987; Thornberry & Krohn, 1997; Thornberry et al., 1994). There is also evidence that the reasons for negative peer relations differ for each gender (Liu & Kaplan, 1996; Pakiz, Reinherz, & Frost, 1992; Rienzi, McMillan, Dickson, Crauthers, McNeill, Pesina, & Mann, 1996; Simons, Johnson, Beaman, Conger, & Whitbeck, 1996; Simpson & Ellis, 1995).

Although forming friendships with peers is important for both male and female adolescents, both the development and constitution of these friendships are very different for each gender (Barnes, Farrell, & Dintcheff, 1997; Bierman & Welsh, 1997; Giordano & Cernkovich, 1997; Giordano, Cernkovich, & Pugh, 1986; Heimer, 1996; White & LaGrange, 1987). Females tend to form stronger bonds and more lasting attachments, and they are generally more concerned about their interpersonal relationships than are males. Females are also much more inclined to be sensitive to the expectations and opinions of others. These gender differences in the formation of close relationships have been shown to exist among both nondelinquent and delinquent adolescents (Giordano et al., 1986; Heimer, 1996) and should be considered when examining the effects of delinquent peers on antisocial behavior. However, the relatively small amount of data on females suggests that more research is necessary to determine the full impact of peers on female delinquency (Giordano & Cernkovich, 1997; White & LaGrange, 1987).

Over the past several decades, a wide range of prevention and intervention programs have been created which focus on reducing juvenile delinquency. The outcomes of these programs have been extremely varied. Some delinquency prevention programs have shown no effect whatsoever in reducing delinquent behavior, some have been relatively successful; others have actually yielded increased levels of delinquency among program participants (Gottfredson & Gottfredson, 1992; Tolan & Guerra, 1994).

It is important to recognize the different genders as separate populations for prevention, intervention, and research purposes, because of the differences that exist between male and female delinquents, and the apparent need for more information about female delinquency. For instance, Fejes-Mendoza et al. (1995) interviewed 40 incarcerated juvenile female offenders and concluded that "preventive and acute treatment models need to be developed for adolescent female delinquents . . . that embrace gender-sensitive constructs" (p. 319). As research on female delinquent offenders progresses, it is becoming more apparent that delinquency intervention and prevention programs need to address gender differences (Ellickson, Saner, & McGuigan, 1997; Fejes-Mendoza et al., 1995; Lifrak, McKay, Rostain, Alterman, & O'Brien, 1997).

Another important area to consider when designing effective delinquency intervention and prevention programs is the impact of deviant peers (Farrington, 1996; Feldman, 1992; O'Donnell et al., 1987). Programs should be designed which "specifically alter the social networks of youths to reduce contact with delinquent peers and increase prosocial relationships" (O'Donnell et al., 1987, p. 261), because of the effect that peers have on juvenile delinquent behavior.

By gathering data on both male and female juvenile offenders, it is possible that a better understanding can be obtained about the processes involved in the development of juvenile delinquency and the effects deviant peers have upon this behavior. This information may enable the creation of comprehensive programs, including those that address peer influences and are tailored to specific gender needs.

Qualitative research methods provide effective ways to gather this data (Fejes-Mendoza et al., 1995; Giordano & Cernkovich, 1997; Leonard, 1982). Qualitative research methods, such as interviewing, have also been shown to be very effective in gaining insight into the social processes and peer relations involved in the formation of delinquent behavior (Cullingford & Morrison, 1997; Goldstein, 1990). Conducting interviews with delinquent juveniles can reveal very important information that cannot be obtained using official documents and court records (Cullingford & Morrison, 1997; Leonard, 1982).

This qualitative study was designed to (1) obtain information concerning both the influence of deviant peers on male and female juvenile criminal behavior and gender differences among adolescents involved in delinquent activities, (2) compare male and female offenders on peer influences and the impact that different relationship styles have on delinquent offending, and (3) provide implications that may assist in the development of effective, gender-sensitive, intervention and prevention programs.

## METHOD

### Setting

Interviews took place at the Hawaii Youth Correctional Facility located on the island of Oahu in the state of Hawaii. Each participant was interviewed individually in a private location where members of the staff could not overhear the conversation. The male participants were interviewed in small visitor cubicles by the entrance to the facility for males. The female participants were interviewed either at a table in the activity yard or in the common room of the facility for females.

### Participants

The initial participants included 11 female and 10 male incarcerated juvenile offenders. One of the female participants requested that her involvement in the project be terminated because she was not comfortable being interviewed. Therefore, the final participants were 10 males and 10 females. Eighteen of the participants were born in Hawaii and all of them spent most of their lives as island residents. The mean age of the female participants was 15.3 years and the mean age of the male participants was 17.5 years. The ethnicity/race of the participants varied. The ethnicity/race of the female participants was: part-Hawaiian (4), Filipino (3), Caucasian (1), Japanese (1), and Samoan (1). The ethnicity/race of the male participants was: part-Hawaiian (4), Filipino (3), Samoan (2), and Black/Caucasian (1). Participants were recruited by social workers employed by the institution and were notified that involvement in the interviewing process was strictly voluntary. Informed consent was obtained from both the superintendent of the institution and each of the participants. The participants were given an oral consent briefing and signed individual consent forms prior to being interviewed.

## Procedure

The data was collected via systematic open-ended questions designed to elicit information concerning the elements involved in the formation of each participant's delinquent behavior. Each interview began with a general appeal for the participant to "tell me about yourself." An effort was made to avoid any leading questions. Emphasis was placed on question prompts targeting peer relations (e.g., "Tell me about your friends," "Tell me about what you talk to them about," "Tell me about how much time you spend with them," "Tell me about what you do when you are hanging out with them"). The interviews were conducted in a conversational style designed to help those being interviewed to feel relaxed and free to express themselves. The interviews were tape-recorded and lasted approximately one hour each. The tapes were then transcribed.

## RESULTS

The interviews were analyzed using Ethnograph v5.0, a computer program designed for the analysis of text-based data. Each transcribed interview was inserted into Ethnograph and segments of interest, defined by the research questions, noted. These segments were coded by marking the segments and assigning a code word to each of them. The frequency of the coded segments was determined. These patterns of coded interview segments formed the basis for the themes in each interview. The themes were divided into categories, using the research questions as an outline, and compared with the other individuals' responses. Comparisons were made by examining the similarities and differences expressed in statements in specific categories. These comparisons were made within and between genders. Utilizing this method of data analysis, two researchers independently conducted category coding of the interview data. The formula used to compute interrater reliability, as suggested by Miles and Huberman (1994), was the total number of agreements divided by total number of agreements plus disagreements within a given category. The reliability scores for each category were then averaged within each gender group. The overall interrater reliability for the categories among females was established at 91% and among the males at 90%.

The data analysis revealed the emergence of a number of clear themes defined by consistent and reoccurring statements. These themes focus on the different elements that affect the formation and continuation of delinquent behaviors in males and females. The responses reflected four distinct themes: peer relationships and influence on deviant behavior, family interactions and deviant behaviors, consequences of delinquent behaviors, and school. There was variation within some of the themes, which was affected by the gender of the person being interviewed.

## Peer Relationships and Influences on Deviant Behaviors

Under the theme of peer relationships, the following categories emerged for males: a tendency to blame peers for deviant behaviors (100%), the need to impress friends (60%), the influence of peers on drug usage (90%), and the psychological "rush" attributed to performing deviant acts (50%). The findings for females under this theme were very different from the males. The categories that emerged for females were: a tendency to blame themselves, rather than their friends for their deviant acts (90%), indication that they were not worried about what their friends thought (60%), and a tendency to blame themselves or their families, rather than their friends for any drug use (70%). One similar category for males and females under this theme was that some peer relationships had positive effects and sometimes assisted in preventing delinquent behaviors (50%).

## Family and Deviant Behaviors

The categories that emerged under the family dynamics theme were also quite different between genders. Males tended not to blame their own deviance on family problems, except in cases where they indicated that their families may have been the cause for their initial dealings with drugs and alcohol (60%). Females, in contrast, were much more inclined to blame their families, rather than their friends for their participation in deviant behaviors (80%). Many of the females also indicated the need to run away from home to escape family problems (70%).

## Consequences of Delinquent Behaviors

Both males and females had similar responses when discussing their feelings towards any potential consequences of their delinquent behaviors. Both genders concluded either that they did not worry about consequences or, if they thought about them, that the consequences did not prevent them from engaging in deviant behaviors (100%).

## School

The themes related to school included whether or not the participants liked school and whether or not they dropped out of school. Males had a tendency to say that they did not like school (70%), and the majority dropped out (70%). Females frequently said that they liked school (70%), or at least that they did well in school, and the majority of them did not drop out (70%). One unanticipated finding was that the majority of both the males (80%) and females (70%) pointed out that school inside the institution was helpful, or that being forced to go to school was a constructive experience.

## DISCUSSION

One of the initial questions of this study was whether female friendship styles and female bonding strongly influence female delinquents' behavior. The data did not support the theory that the nature of female relationships makes them more prone to peer influences. This conclusion is based upon replies given by females when talking about their peer relationships and other influences on their deviant behaviors.

First, the females in this study readily acknowledged that they got into trouble by themselves as well as with their friends. They tended to put most of the blame for their own delinquent behavior upon themselves or their families rather than upon their friends. One possible explanation of this finding is that their peer relationships did not have as much influence on their deviant behavior as may have been expected by the nature of female friendship formation, which suggests stronger bonding patterns and more intimate friendships than males. The females in this study were quick to note that they did not worry about what their friends thought. Therefore, the conclusion may be drawn that the delinquent behavior of the females did not seem to be dependent upon the opinions or actions of their friends and they were not necessarily seeking peer approval when participating in negative behavior.

Another sentiment expressed by several of the girls was that they felt as if they were loners or had few friends. These girls did not indicate that they were linked with intimate groups that were tied with strong relationship bonds, but instead they implied that there was a lack of peer influence.

The findings did support the influence of peer relationships on males, when engaging in deviant behaviors. The male participants frequently attributed part of the responsibility for their delinquent actions to their friends. This was also true in sentiments expressed concerning the use of drugs and alcohol, activities which the males indicated were highly influenced by peers. This male tendency to blame their friends for their actions was in sharp contrast to what females said about their motivation.

Another finding about the males that was absent from the females' expressions was the apparent need to impress peers. Their concern about what their friends think suggest that males need to have some sort of approval from friends when engaging in delinquent activities. The need to impress others is also in direct contrast to the female participants' rejection of concern associated with their friends' opinions of them.

Some males talked about their different sets of friends, some of whom influence engagement in delinquent activities, while others do not. This finding indicates that some males may be associated with more than one peer network or loosely formed groups of peers, and these groups may have varying attitudes towards delinquency.

Although most of the male and female study participants had lived in separated or malfunctioning families, the data indicates that family problems had a greater effect on the manifestation and continuation of female delinquency than male delinquency. Females seemed to react to family problem situations by exhibiting personal delinquent behavior. The females were substantially more likely than males to blame their families or themselves, rather than their peers, for negative behavior patterns. This was especially apparent in the females' frequent assessment of family problems as their reason for drug use. Although some of the males blamed their families for early contact with drugs, they blamed their friends for the continuation or escalation of drug usage. Males tended not to blame family problems for their other delinquent activities and generally did not exhibit the flight patterns shown by females. Running away from home was a common female response to negative family environments and this often led them into situations that aggravated their delinquent behavior.

There seemed to be no gender differences in the attitudes expressed concerning the consequences of delinquent behaviors. Both males and females either denied having any concern about the consequences of their delinquent actions or admitted that they thought about it sometimes, but these thoughts did not deter their negative behaviors. These findings would suggest that both males and females had little immediate concern about social consequences and societal norms associated with their delinquent behavior. Some of the male attitudes concerning peer relationships might help to explain their lack of concern for consequences. The males talked both about the rush they felt when engaging in delinquent actions and about the need to impress their friends. These elements could be construed to be more important to the males than the consequences of their negative actions, and, therefore, fear of consequences did not curtail their delinquent behavior.

The total disregard of consequences for their deviant actions expressed by both the males and females has implications for the justice system, which relies on punishment as a deterrent. It is apparent that for this group of delinquents, fear of consequences did not deter their delinquent activities. Studies are needed to explore how the juvenile justice system could become more effective in preventing antisocial behaviors of delinquents whose fear of consequences is ineffective as a deterrent.

There were several findings associated with school for both males and females. However, it is difficult to deduce from these findings the relationship between peer influences and school. First, there was no evidence that academic aspirations of peers affected either the males or the females. The females did seem to have a better attitude about the positive value of school. This was reflected in their lower dropout rates and in the response by some females that either they liked school or that they did well in school. The males were much more likely to express a dislike for school and their dropout rates were higher. It is interesting to note that both genders frequently exhibited much more positive attitudes about school attendance, when it was required of them in the correctional institution environment.

Although the hypothesis concerning peer influences being a key component in female delinquent behavior was not supported by this study, pertinent information was obtained. Historically, studies of delinquent behaviors have primarily focused on males. The inclusion of females in these studies is vital. Otherwise, it is difficult to understand what is necessary to build effective gender-specific intervention/prevention programs. By gaining an understanding of which risks may be more influential in inducing delinquent behaviors in each sex, programs can be designed which target gender-specific risks and are more effective in preventing and treating delinquent behavior.

The findings in this study indicate that programs designed for girls should consider the risks associated with family dynamics. There has been some support for the effectiveness of family-based interventions, which are aimed at improving parenting style and family relations to produce a more positive and healthy environment (Henggler, 1991;

Henggler, Melton, & Smith, 1992; Tolan & Guerra, 1994). These types of interventions can include both parent training and family therapy.

Programs designed for males need to consider the impact that peer relationships have on the continuation of delinquent behaviors. There is some evidence of the relative effectiveness of peer-related programs. In the St. Louis Experiment (Feldman, 1992), youths were divided into groups of referred youths (those who exhibited problem behaviors) and nonreferred youths (those who did not have behavioral problems). It was found that the antisocial behavior of the referred youths significantly declined when mixed with prosocial peer groups, but there was no change in the behavior of the referred youths who were not exposed to the prosocial group. Mentoring programs, which focus on protective elements related to prosocial bonding, have also been shown to be somewhat successful in reducing problem behaviors (Howell, 1995). Ideally, designing programs focusing on the risks associated with peer influences will assist in reducing delinquent behaviors.

Another important variable, when designing programs for both genders, is the role of school and education. In this study, it was found that a number of the participants enjoyed school during their incarceration and were excited about the prospect of graduating. The reason they were even finishing school, in many cases, was the requirement of school within the institutional setting without outside distractions. Prevention programs need to carefully address education concerns and consideration should be given to tailoring them to be gender-sensitive. These findings can contribute to the ongoing effort in constructing effective delinquency prevention and intervention programs. Studies with a gender comparison help to determine the direction these programs should take.

Several limitations that existed within this study should be noted. First, the selection of participants in this study was quite limited because of the small number of incarcerated delinquents in Hawaii. This resulted in an unavoidable difference between the mean age of the females (15.3 years) and the mean age of the males (17.5 years). It was clear during the interviewing process that the males were much more willing to speak without being prompted and felt more comfortable in the presence of the interviewer. The older age (and presumed greater maturity) of the males probably helped them feel more comfortable than the females did in talking about their lives and revealing information.

The discrepancy in the mean ages between males and females could be a major influence in the findings related to peer influences on delinquent behaviors. It is possible that because the females were younger, they had not yet reached an age where peer contact strongly influences negative behavior patterns. Instead, family dysfunction was primarily associated with the delinquent behaviors of younger females. To determine whether age is a component in relation to peer influence on female delinquent behaviors, future research will need to sample a population of older female delinquents.

Another difference that existed between the genders was that the males tended to be incarcerated for more serious offenses than the females. This could help to explain some of the gender differences in relation to peer contact and influences. The older males had more years of experience with increasingly serious deviant behaviors and more opportunities to become involved with deviant peer groups than the younger females.

The fact that all of the participants in the study were incarcerated could also be a limitation. It is possible that different themes would result among adolescents who are not in correctional facilities. Additional studies need to examine the friendship formation patterns of both incarcerated and nonincarcerated female delinquents to determine whether or not there are differences in relation to peer and family influences.

To address these limitations, future research should continue to focus on the gender differences associated with these behaviors. It is apparent that males and females may be affected by different risks that facilitate negative behavior patterns. It is also apparent that there are some delinquent actions independent of gender. Understanding and comparing the differences and similarities may enable inferences to be drawn, which will lead to the reduction of criminal behaviors in adolescents.

## REFERENCES

Barnes, G., Farrell, M., & Dintcheff, B. (1997). Family socialization effects on alcohol abuse and related problem behaviors among female and male adolescents. In R. Wilsnack & S. Wilsnack (Eds.), *Gender and alcohol: Individual and social perspectives* (pp. 156-175). New Brunswick, NJ: Rutgers Center of Alcohol Studies.

Bierman, K. (1997). Social relationship deficits. In E. Mash & L. Terdal (Eds.), *Assessment of childhood disorders* (pp. 328-365). New York: Guilford Press.

Calhoun, G., Jurgens, J., & Chen, F. (1993). The neophyte female delinquent: A review of the literature. *Adolescence, 28*, 461-471.

Chung, H., & Elias, M. (1996). Patterns of adolescent involvement in problem behaviors: Relationship to self-efficacy, social competence, and life events. *American Journal of Community Psychology, 24*, 771-784.

Cullingford, C., & Morrison, J. (1997). Peer group pressure within and outside school. *British Educational Research Journal, 23*, 61-80.

Ellickson, P., Saner, H., & McGuigan, K. (1997). Profiles of violent youth: Substance use and other concurrent problems. *American Journal of Public Health, 87*, 985-991.

Elliot, D. S., & Menard, S. (1996). Delinquent friends and delinquent behavior: Temporal and developmental patterns. In Hawkins, D. J. (Ed.), *Delinquency and crime: Current theories* (pp. 28-67). New York, NY: Cambridge.

Farrington, D. P. (1996). The explanation and prevention of youthful offending. In D. J. Hawkins (Ed.), *Delinquency and crime: Current theories* (pp. 68-148). New York: Cambridge University Press.

Fejes-Mendoza, K., Miller, D., & Eppler, R. (1995). Portraits of dysfunction: Criminal, educational, and family profiles of juvenile female offenders. *Education and Treatment of Children, 18*, 309-321.

Feldman, R. A. (1992). The St. Louis experiment: Effective treatment of antisocial youths in prosocial peer groups. In J. McCord & R. Tremblay (Eds.), *Preventing antisocial behavior: Interventions from birth through adolescents* (pp. 233-252). New York: Guilford Press.

Giordano, P., & Cernkovich, A. (1997). Gender and antisocial behavior. In D. M. Stoff, J. Breiling, & J. D. Maser (Eds.), *Handbook of antisocial behavior* (pp. 496-510). New York: Wiley.

Giordano, P., Cernkovich, A., & Pugh, M. (1986). Friendships and delinquency. *American Journal of Sociology, 91*, 1171-1202.

Goldstein, A. (1990). *Delinquents on delinquency*. Champaign, IL: Research Press.

Gottfredson, D. C., & Gottfredson, G. D. (1992). Theory-guided investigation: Three field experiments. In J. McCord & R. E. Tremblay (Eds.), *Preventing antisocial behavior: Interventions from birth through adolescence* (pp. 311-329). New York: Guilford Press.

Heimer, K. (1996). Gender, interaction, and delinquency: Testing a theory of differential social control. *Social Psychology Quarterly, 59*, 39-61.

Henggeler, S. W. (1991). Multidimensional causal models of delinquent behavior and their implications for treatment. In R. Cohen & A. Siegel (Eds.), *Context and development* (211-231). Hillsdale, NJ: Lawrence Erlbaum Associates.

Henggeler, S., Melton, G., & Smith, L. (1992). Family preservation using multisystematic therapy. *Journal of Consulting and Clinical Psychology, 22*, 132-141.

Howell, J. C. (1995). *Guide for implementing the comprehensive strategy for serious, violent, and chronic juvenile offenders*. Washington, DC: U.S. Department of Justice, Office of Justice Programs, Office of Juvenile Justice and Delinquency Prevention.

Leonard, E. (1982). *A critique of criminal theory: Women, crime, and society*. New York: Longman.

Lifrak, P. D., McKay, J. R., Rostain, A., Alterman, A. I., & O'Brien, C. P. (1997). Relationship of perceived competencies, perceived social support, and gender to substance use in young adolescents. *Journal of the American Academy of Child and Adolescent Psychiatry 35*, 933-940.

Liu, X., & Kaplan, H. (1995). Gender-related differences surrounding initiation and escalation of alcohol and other substance use/abuse. *Deviant Behavior, 17*, 71-106.

Lowry, R., Sleet, D., Duncan, C., Powell, K., & Kolbe, L. (1995). Adolescents at risk for violence. *Educational Psychology Review, 7*, 7-39.

Miles, M. B., & Huberman, A. M. (1994). *Qualitative data analysis: An expanded sourcebook* (2nd ed.). Thousand Oaks, CA: Sage.

Miller, D., Trapani, C., Fejes-Mendoza, K., Eggleston, C., & Dwiggins, D. (1995). Adolescent female offenders: Unique considerations. *Adolescence, 30*, 428-435.

Molidor, C. E. (1996). Female gang members: A profile of aggression and victimization. *Social Work, 41*, 251-257.

Mulvey, E. P., & Woolard, J. L. (1997). Themes for consideration in future research on prevention and intervention with antisocial behaviors. In D. M. Stoff, J. Breiling, & J. D. Maser (Eds.), *Handbook of antisocial behavior* (pp. 454-459). New York: Wiley.

O'Donnell, C., Manos, J., & Chesney-Lind, M. (1987). Diversion and neighborhood delinquency programs in open settings: A social network interpretation. In E. K. Morris & C. J. Braukman (Eds.), *Behavioral approaches to crime and delinquency: Application, research and theory* (pp. 251-269). New York: Plenum Press.

O'Donnell, C. R., & Tharp, R. G. (1990). Community intervention guided by theoretical development. In A. S. Bellack, M. Hersen, & A. E. Kasdin (Eds.), *International handbook of behavior modification and therapy* (pp. 251-266). New York: Plenum Press.

Pakiz, B., Reinherz, H. Z., & Frost, A. K. (1992). Antisocial behavior in adolescence: A community study. *Journal of Early Adolescence, 12*, 300-313.

Rienzi, B., McNeill, K., Mcmillin, J., Pesina, M., Dickson, C., Mann, E., & Crauthers, D. (1996). Gender differences regarding peer influence and attitude toward substance abuse. *Journal of Drug Education, 26*, 339-347.

Siegel, L.J., & Senna, J.J. (1981). *Juvenile delinquency: Theory, practice, and law*. St. Paul, MN: West Publishing Co.

Simons, R., Johnson, C., Beaman, J., Conger, R., & Whitbeck, L. (1996). Parents and peer group as mediators of the effect of community structure on adolescent problem behavior. *American Journal of Community Psychology, 24*, 145-171.

Simpson, S., & Elis, L. (1995). Doing gender: Sorting out the caste and crime conundrum. *Criminology, 33*, 47-81.

Snyder, H., & Sickmund, M. (1999). *Juvenile offenders and victims: 1999 national report*. Washington, DC: U.S. Department of Justice, Office of Justice Programs, Office of Juvenile Justice and Delinquency Prevention.

Thornberry, T. P., & Krohn, M. D. (1997). Peers, drug use, and delinquency. In D. M. Stoff, J. Breiling, & J. D. Maser (Eds.), *Handbook of antisocial behavior*. (pp. 218-233). New York: Wiley.

Thornberry, T. P., Lizotte, A. J., Krohn, M. D., Farnworth, M., & Jang, S. J. (1994). Delinquent peers, beliefs, and delinquent behavior: A longitudinal test of interactional theory. *Criminology, 32*, 47-80.

Tolan, H. P., & Guerra, N. G. (1994). Prevention of delinquency: Current status and issues. *Applied and Preventive Psychology, 3*, 251-273.

Warr, M. (1993). Parents, peers, and delinquency. *Social Forces, 72*, 247-264.

White, H., & La Grange, R. (1987). An assessment of gender effects in self report delinquency. *Sociological Focus, 20*, 195-213.

# Culture, Peers, and Delinquency: Implications for the Community-Peer Model of Delinquency

Clifford R. O'Donnell

*University of Hawaii*

**SUMMARY.** A community-peer model of delinquency shows how family, school, and neighborhood variables affect adolescent peers groups, which then affect the likelihood of juvenile delinquency. The findings on culture and gender presented in the studies in this volume are discussed in relation to this model. Overall, the findings support the community-peer model for males across the various cultural groups. Incarcerated females, however, attributed their delinquency more to family than to

Clifford R. O'Donnell, PhD, Professor of Psychology, University of Hawaii, serves as Director of the Community and Culture Graduate Program at the University. He has published extensively on such topics as delinquency prevention, firearm deaths among children, and youth, social networks, programs for at-risk youths, community intervention, culturally-compatible forms of community development, and education and employment in community psychology. Professor O'Donnell has received awards as an "Outstanding Professor," and for his "Dedication and Support" toward the prevention of violence, and "Outstanding Contributions to Education and Training in Community Research and Action."

Address correspondence to: Clifford R. O'Donnell, Department of Psychology, University of Hawaii, 2430 Campus Road, Honolulu, HI 96822 (E-mail: cliffo@hawaii.edu).

[Haworth co-indexing entry note]: "Culture, Peers, and Delinquency: Implications for the Community-Peer Model of Delinquency." O'Donnell, Clifford R. Co-published simultaneously in *Journal of Prevention & Intervention in the Community* (The Haworth Press, Inc.) Vol. 25, No. 2, 2003, pp. 79-87; and: *Culture, Peers, and Delinquency* (ed: Clifford R. O'Donnell) The Haworth Press, Inc., 2003, pp. 79-87. Single or multiple copies of this article are available for a fee from The Haworth Document Delivery Service [1-800-HAWORTH, 9:00 a.m. - 5:00 p.m. (EST). E-mail address: docdelivery@haworthpress.com].

10.1300/J005v25n02_06

peers. Additional research is needed to clarify this difference. Implications for assessment, prevention, and intervention are discussed. *[Article copies available for a fee from The Haworth Document Delivery Service: 1-800-HAWORTH. E-mail address: <docdelivery@haworthpress.com> Website: <http://www.HaworthPress.com> © 2003 by The Haworth Press, Inc. All rights reserved.]*

**KEYWORDS.** Culture, peers, delinquency, community, gender, activity settings

Interest in juvenile delinquency has a long history (Binder, Geis, & Bruce, 2001) with considerable recent attention on youth violence (Gullotta, Adams, & Montemayor, 1998; O'Donnell, 1995, 2001), gangs (Huff, 2002), and the implications of risk and protective factors (Loeber & Farrington, 1998, 2001). Theoretical attempts at understanding have ranged from genetics to the structure of society (Binder, Geis, & Bruce, 2001).

DiLalla and Gottesman (1991) reviewed the genetic and biological evidence for criminality in adults and juveniles. A comparison of adults and juveniles found strong support for both genetic and environmental components in adult criminality but, in contrast, delinquent behaviors "were not significantly heritable" (DiLalla & Gottesman, 1991, p. 126), suggesting the importance of environmental variables for delinquency.

Among the environmental variables that have been extensively studied are those related to family, school, and neighborhood. They have been combined into risk and protective factors to predict the likelihood of delinquency (e.g., Brier, 1989; Hawkins, Catalano, & Miller, 1992; Howell, 1995; Saner & Ellickson, 1996). While providing important information, risk and protective factors alone do not show how delinquency occurs.

A community-peer model illustrates how family, school, and neighborhood risk and protective factors influence contact with peers, and how peers can serve as a pathway to delinquency (O'Donnell, 1998, 2000). Peers are the key factor in this model because adolescents are at an age when they are most receptive to peer influence (Cullingford & Morrison, 1997), most delinquent activity is committed in groups (Emler, Reicher, & Ross, 1987; Erickson & Jensen, 1977; Gold, 1970; West & Farrington, 1973), high-risk adolescents reward peer deviant behavior (Dishion, McCord, & Poulin, 1999), and participation in activity settings with high-risk and delinquent peers is one of the best predictors of delinquency (Arnold & Hughes, 1999; Lyon, Henggeler, & Hall, 1992; O'Donnell, 1992; O'Donnell, Manos, & Chesney-Lind, 1987; Paterson & Yoerger, 1997; Poole & Rigoli, 1979; White, Pandina, & LaGrange, 1987).

This community-peer model suggests that family, school, and neighborhood factors affect the risk for delinquency by facilitating or inhibiting contact with different peer groups. For example, family risk factors that are more likely to increase contact with high-risk peers include parents with alcohol, drug, psychotic, or criminal problems (Dembo, Williams, Wothke, Schmeidler, & Brown, 1992), lack of parental supervision (Wilson, 1980), and child abuse, neglect, or rejection (Maxfield & Widom, 1996; Scudder, Blount, Heide, & Silverman, 1993; Widom, 1989). These family problems can increase the amount of time youths spend outside the home and, thereby, increase the potential for association and influence of delinquent peers (O'Donnell et al., 1987; Paterson & Yoerger, 1997; Simons, Johnson, Beaman, Conger, & Whitbeck, 1996). Conversely, familial attachment can decrease involvement with delinquent peers (Warr, 1993).

Similarly, youths with poor academic performance (Cornwall & Bawden, 1992; Meltzer, Levine, Karniski, Palfrey, & Clarke, 1984; Wilgosh & Paitich, 1982), school disciplinary referrals, or truancy are more likely to have contact with other youths with the same problems (e.g., Dishion, Patterson, & Kavanagh, 1992). Youths with family and school problems may be protected if they live in neighborhoods with low rates of crime and drug abuse, and the presence of activities supervised by responsible adults.

Conversely, youths living in neighborhoods with easy access to firearms (O'Donnell, 1995), a lack of adult social ties and adult-supervised activities (Schwendinger & Schwendinger, 1982), and peers involved with drug abuse, drug sales, gangs, and criminal activities (Figueira-McDonough, 1993; Griffin, Scheier, Borvin, Diaz, & Miller, 1999; Gottfredson, McNeil, & Gottfredson, 1991; Sampson, Raudenbush, & Earls, 1997; Shannon, 1988) are more likely to participate in activity settings where criminal behavior occurs in the routine course of their everyday lives (O'Donnell & Tharp, 1990; O'Donnell, Tharp, & Wilson, 1993). In these neighborhoods, youths may be protected by attachment to family and by school success (Dishion, Patterson, Stoolmiller, & Skinner, 1991; Poole & Rigoli, 1979).

While this community-peer model considers the effects of family, school, neighborhoods, and peers on delinquency, the possible effects of culture are not mentioned. One of the goals of the studies presented in this issue was to examine the possible effects of culture based on ethnicity and race. Acosta (this volume) compared groups of Caucasian, East Asian, South-East Asian, and Polynesian/Micronesian youths and found strong support for a youth culture that crossed ethnic and racial boundaries. All of the groups had friends from other ethnic and racial groups in similar proportions. There also were no differences among the groups in age, gender, or number of close friends. In addition, each group was similar in their degree of attachment to peers, the influence of their peers, and their degree of involvement with their own group. Regardless of their ethnic or racial group, each reported trust in their friends and selected their friends as the first ones they would turn to with their problems.

The profound changes in Japanese society since World War II, leading to the emergence of a youth culture in Japan, is documented by Yamamiya (this volume). Ironically, cultural changes are reducing the influence of traditional culture among the young. As family and school problems have increased, peers have become more prominent in the lives of Japanese youth. Yamamiya's report of less adult supervision of adolescents and greater peer influence and attachment is similar to the characteristics of youth culture in the United States. These characteristics also were found among the Vietnamese immigrants in Hawaii (Thai, this volume).

The strong support for the influence of a youth culture among Japanese youth in Japan and Vietnamese immigrants and Caucasian, East Asian, South-East Asian, and Polynesian/Micronesian youth in Hawaii, found in these studies, suggests that any influence of ethnic culture on delinquency is through their effect on peers, at least among these ethnic and racial groups. Among the Vietnamese immigrants, immigration affects family life as youth adapt American lifestyles. The conflicts between generations provide the content in the process of family influence on peer relationships (Thai, this volume). For example, arguments at home and child abuse increase the likelihood of youth spending free time away from the home and in the company of peers with similar problems. Conversely, parents who are able to facilitate youth activities with responsible adult supervision may provide some protection for their children.

Ethnic cultures may affect peer relationships through the activities they do or do not support. Time spent in solitary activities, such as reading, is associated with lower group delinquency rates, while greater time spent in activities with peers, such as unsupervised partying and concert attendance, is associated with higher rates of group delinquency (Acosta, this volume ). As Tharp (this volume) noted, learning takes place in joint activity within cultures. Activity setting theory suggests that delinquent activity, like any other behavior, is a function of the characteristics of the particular activity setting, including the partici- pants (O'Donnell & Tharp, 1990; O'Donnell, Tharp, & Wilson, 1993; Tharp, this volume).

Peer relationships are formed, in part, by activities (Acosta, this vol- ume) and activities are influenced by peer relationships. The commu- nity-peer model, in which peers mediate the effects of families, schools, and neighborhoods on delinquency, is based on activity setting theory (O'Donnell & Tharp, 1990; O'Donnell et al., 1993). Families, schools, and neighborhoods, including those with ethnic traditions, can facilitate or inhibit delinquency by affecting activities with peers and the peer re- lationships that form from these activities.

The studies in this collection provide support for the community-peer model, at least regarding male delinquency. The questionnaire and fo- cus group data presented on different ethnic and racial groups by Acosta, the interviews of the Vietnamese community by Thai, the inter- views with incarcerated boys by Galbavy, and the socio-cultural-histor- ical analysis by Yamamiya, indicate the primary importance of peers in delinquency. Incarcerated boys sought approval from their friends and blamed them for their delinquency (Galbavy, this volume), while Japa- nese youth, especially those with the highest delinquency rates, also blamed their friends for their offenses (Yamamiya, this volume).

A important exception to the support for the community-peer model is the finding that incarcerated girls indicated the importance of fami- lies, rather than peers, on their delinquent behavior (Galbavy, this vol- ume). These girls saw themselves as loners with few friends. Additional studies are needed to determine if this difference is related to gender, age, or other characteristics of these individuals.

The community-peer model has important implications for the as- sessment of juvenile offenders and the prevention of delinquency. The model shows that assessment of the individual offender is insufficient and information about families, schools, neighborhoods, and peers is also required. The mediation of delinquency by peers in this model sug- gests that delinquency prevention programs should assess their effect on their participants' peer network. Prevention efforts that focus on families, schools, and neighborhoods can be more effective if they af- fect peer activity settings and networks. Tharp (this volume) suggests that increasing the participation of responsible adults in youth activity settings can reduce peer influence, increase adult supervision, and help to prevent delinquency.

In addition, there is an important need to develop delinquency prevention programs designed to alter association with high-risk peers (Tolan & Guerra, 1994). Prevention programs and school policies, such as tracking systems, detention, and suspension, often bring high-risk youth together and thereby increase the risk for delinquency (O'Donnell et al., 1987), while programs that reduce the association among high-risk youth can also reduce delinquency (Feldman, 1992). Reducing contact among high-risk peers is particularly important in intervention programs for youths who have already engaged in delinquent behavior (Tharp, this volume).

## REFERENCES

Acosta, J. (2003). The effects of cultural differences on peer group relationships. In C.R. O'Donnell (Ed.), *Culture, peers, and delinquency.* Binghamton, NY: The Haworth Press, Inc.

Arnold, M. E., & Hughes, J. N. (1999). First do no harm: Adverse effects of grouping deviant youth for skills training. *Journal of School Psychology, 37,* 99-115.

Binder, A., Geis, G., & Bruce, D.D. Jr. (2001). *Juvenile delinquency: Historical, cultural, and legal perspectives* (3rd ed.). Cincinnati: Anderson.

Brier, N. (1989). The relationship between learning disability and delinquency: A review and reappraisal. *Journal of Learning Disabilities, 22,* 546-553.

Cornwall, A., & Bawden, H. N. (1992). Reading disabilities and aggression. A critical review. *Journal of Learning Disabilities, 25,* 281-288.

Cullingford, C., & Morrison, J. (1997). Peer group pressure within and outside school. *British Educational Research Journal, 23,* 61-80.

Dembo, R., Williams, L., Wothke, W., Schmeidler, J., & Brown, C. H. (1992). The role of family factors, physical abuse, and sexual victimization experiences in high-risk youths' alcohol and other drug use and delinquency: A longitudinal model. *Violence and Victims, 7,* 245-266.

DiLalla, L. F., & Gottesman, I. I. (1991). Biological and genetic contributors to violence–Widom's untold tale. *Psychological Bulletin, 109,* 125-129.

Dishion, T. J., McCord, J., & Poulin, F. (1999). When interventions harm: Peer groups and problem behavior. *American Psychologist, 54,* 755-764.

Dishion, T. J., Patterson, G. R., & Kavanagh, K. A. (1992). An experimental test of the coercion model: Linking theory, measurement, and intervention. In J. McCord & R. Tremblay (Eds.), *Preventing antisocial behavior: Interventions from birth through adolescence* (pp. 253-282). New York: Guilford Press.

Dishion, T. J., Patterson, G. R., Stoolmiller, M., & Skinner, M. L. (1991). Family, school, and behavioral antecedents to early adolescent involvement with antisocial peers. *Developmental Psychology, 27,* 172-180.

Emler, N., Reicher, S., & Ross, A. (1987). The social context of delinquent conduct. *Journal of Child Psychology and Psychiatry, 28*, 99-109.

Erickson, M. L., & Jensen, G. F. (1977). Delinquency is still group behavior: Toward revitalizing the group premise in the sociology of deviance. *Journal of Criminal Law and Criminology, 68*, 262-277.

Feldman, R. A. (1992). The St. Louis experiment: Effective treatment of antisocial youths in prosocial peer groups. In J. McCord & R. Tremblay (Eds.), *Preventing antisocial behavior: Interventions from birth through adolescents* (pp. 233-252). New York: Guilford Press.

Figueira-McDonough, J. (1993). Residence, dropping out, and delinquency rates. *Deviant Behavior: An Interdisciplinary Journal, 14*, 109-132.

Galbavy, R. J. (2003). Juvenile delinquency: Peer influences, gender differences and prevention. In C.R. O'Donnell (Ed.), *Culture, peers, and delinquency*. Binghamton, NY: The Haworth Press, Inc.

Gold, M. (1970). *Delinquent behavior in an American city*. Belmont, CA: Brooks/Cole.

Gottfredson, D. C., McNeil, R. J., III, & Gottfredson, G. D. (1991). Social area influences on delinquency: A multilevel analysis. *Journal of Research in Crime and Delinquency, 28*, 197-226.

Griffin, K. Scheier, L., Borvin, G. J., Diaz, T., & Miller, N. (1999). Interpersonal aggression in urban minority youth: Mediators of perceived neighborhood, peer, and parental influences. *Journal of Community Psychology, 27*, 281-298.

Gullotta, T. P., Adams, G. R., & Montemayor, R. (Eds.) (1998). *Delinquent violent youth: Theory and interventions*. Thousand Oaks, CA: Sage.

Hawkins, J., Catalano, R., & Miller, J. Y. (1992). Risk and protective factors for alcohol and other drug problems in adolescence and early adulthood: Implications for substance abuse prevention. *Psychological Bulletin, 69*, 248-268.

Howell, J. D. (Ed.) (1995). *Guide to implementing the comprehensive strategy for serious, violent, and chronic juvenile offenders*. Washington, DC: Office of Juvenile Justice and Delinquency Prevention.

Huff, C. R. (Ed.) (2002). *Gangs in America*. Thousand Oaks, CA: Sage.

Loeber, R., & Farrington, D. P. (Eds.) (1998). *Serious and violent juvenile offenders: Risk factors and successful interventions*. Thousand Oaks, CA: Sage.

Loeber, R., & Farrington, D. P. (Eds.) (2001). *Child delinquents: Development, intervention, and service needs*. Thousand Oaks, CA: Sage.

Lyon, J. M., Henggeler, S. W., & Hall, J. A. (1992). The family relations, peer relations, and criminal activities of Caucasian and Hispanic-American gang members. *Journal of Abnormal Child Psychology, 20*, 439-449.

Maxfield, M. G., & Widom, C. S. (1996). The cycle of violence: Revisited 6 years later. *Archives of Pediatric and Adolescent Medicine, 150*, 390-395.

Meltzer, L. J., Levine, M. D., Karniski, W., Palfrey, J. S., & Clarke, S. (1984). An analysis of the learning styles of adolescent delinquents. *Journal of Learning Disabilities, 17*, 600-608.

O'Donnell, C. R. (1992). The interplay of theory and practice in delinquency prevention: From behavior modification to activity settings. In J. McCord & R. Tremblay (Eds.), *Preventing antisocial behavior: Interventions from birth through adolescence* (pp. 209-232). New York: Guilford Press.

O'Donnell, C. R. (1995). Firearm deaths among children and youth. *American Psychologist, 50*, 771-776.

O'Donnell, C. R. (1998, May). *Peers and delinquency: Implications for prevention and intervention.* Presentation at the Violence and Youth: Overcoming the Odds: Helping Children and Families at Risk Conference, Miami, FL.

O'Donnell, C. R. (2000). *Youth with disabilities in the juvenile justice system: A literature review.* Clemson, SC: Consortium on Children, Families, and the Law, Clemson University, Institute on Family and Neighborhood Life.

O'Donnell, C. R. (Ed.) (2001). School violence (special issue). *Law & Policy, 23.*

O'Donnell, C. R., Manos, M. J., & Chesney-Lind, M. (1987). Diversion and neighborhood delinquency programs in open settings: A social network interpretation. In E. K. Morris & C. J. Braukman (Eds.), *Behavioral approaches to crime and delinquency: Application, research and theory* (pp. 251-269). New York: Plenum Press.

O'Donnell, C. R., & Tharp, R. G. (1990). Community intervention guided by theoretical developments. In A. S. Bellack, M. Hersen, & A. E. Kazdin (Eds.), *International handbook of behavior modification and therapy*, 2nd Edition (pp. 251-266). New York: Plenum Press.

O'Donnell, C. R., Tharp, R. G., & Wilson, K. (1993). Activity settings as the unit of analysis: A theoretical basis for community intervention and development. *American Journal of Community Psychology, 21*, 501-520.

Patterson, G. R., & Yoerger, K. (1997). A developmental model for late-onset delinquency. In W. Osgood (Ed.), *Motivation and delinquency* (pp. 118-177). Lincoln, NE: University of Nebraska Press.

Poole, E. D., & Rigoli, R. M. (1979). Parental support, delinquent friends, and delinquency: A test of interaction effects. *Journal of Law and Criminology, 70*, 188-194.

Sampson, R. J., Raudenbush, S. W., & Earls, F. (1997). Neighborhoods and violent crime: A multilevel study of collective efficacy. *Science, 277*, 918-924.

Saner, H., & Ellickson, P. (1996). Concurrent risk factors for adolescent violence. *Journal of Adolescent Health, 19*, 94-103.

Schwendinger, H., & Schwendinger, J. (1982). The paradigmatic crisis in delinquency theory. *Crime and Social Justice, 17*, 70-78.

Scudder, R. G., Blount, W. R., Heide, K. M., & Silverman, I. J. (1993). Important links between child abuse, neglect, and delinquency. *International Journal of Offender Therapy and Comparative Criminology, 37*, 315-323.

Shannon, L. W. (1988). *Criminal career continuity: Its social context.* New York: Human Sciences Press.

Simons, R. L., Johnson, C., Beaman, J., Conger, R. D., & Whitbeck, L. B. (1996). Parents and peer group as mediators of the effect of community structure on adolescent problem behavior. *American Journal of Community Psychology, 24*, 145-171.

Thai, N. D. (2003). Vietnamese youth gangs in Honolulu. In C.R. O'Donnell (Ed.), *Culture, peers, and delinquency.* Binghamton, NY: The Haworth Press, Inc.

Tharp, R. G. (2003). Juvenile delinquency: Culture and community, person and society, theory and research. In C.R. O'Donnell (Ed.), *Culture, peers, and delinquency.* Binghamton, NY: The Haworth Press, Inc.

Tolan, P. H., & Guerra, N. G. (1994). Prevention of delinquency: Current status and issues. *Applied & Preventive Psychology, 3*, 251-273.

Warr, M. (1993). Parents, peers, and delinquency. *Social Forces, 72*, 247-264.

West, D. J., & Farrington, D. P. (1973). *Who becomes delinquent?* London: Heineman Educational Books.

White, H. R., Pandina, R. J., & LaGrange, R. L. (1987). Longitudinal predictors of serious substance use and delinquency. *Criminology, 25*, 715-740.

Widom, C. S. (1989). Does violence beget violence? A critical examination of the literature. *Psychological Bulletin, 106*, 3-28.

Wilgosh, L., & Paitich, D. (1982). Delinquency and learning disabilities: More evidence. *Journal of Learning Disabilities, 15*, 278-279.

Wilson, H. (1980). Parental supervision: A neglected aspect of delinquency. *British Journal of Criminology, 20*, 203-235.

Yamamiya, Y. (2003). Juvenile delinquency in Japan. In C.R. O'Donnell (Ed.), *Culture, peers, and delinquency.* Binghamton, NY: The Haworth Press, Inc.

# Index